INSIDE MY WORLD

*It is our uniqueness as individuals
that makes our lives so precious*

Larry Johnson

ISBN: 1449971725
ISBN-13: 9781449971724
Library of Congress Control Number: 2009913926

TO MOM

A TRULY REMARKABLE WOMAN

TABLE OF CONTENTS

ACKNOWLEDGEMENTS

I have many people to thank for bringing this book to reality. It has passed under the scrutiny of my brother Jim, and his professional journalist's eye, my sister, Dorothy, who has a marvelous memory for the correct spelling of names of people and places.

I am grateful to Doris, one of Dorothy's very best friends, for providing me with some fascinating facts about Riverview.

My thanks go also to Jim, Dorothy, Dorothy's daughter, Maureen, my three daughters Luana, Shirley and Ana and grand-daughter Tatiana for helping to select the photographs that I have sprinkled throughout the book, and to son-in-law Sam for scanning and copying them multiple times.

Thanks to George, Marty, Wanda and Pompeyo for sharing with me some of their fondest recollections of are youth.

I also want to acknowledge and thank my dear friend BJ for her very thorough and careful proof-reading of the manuscript in its early stages.

There's not a dangling participle that would ever get away from BJ.

Finally, my profoundest gratitude goes to Dr. Annie Riedling whose incredible enthusiasm and excitement over this project has truly amazed me and kept me motivated and committed to completing it. From more than a thousand miles away, she has reviewed and corrected my text, helped me select the cover design, the type face, the spacing and the positioning of the pictures. And all throughout she was ever ready to offer so many kind words of encouragement and support.

Thank you all.

LPJ

FOREWORD

I have been blind all of my life (from the age of six months). Indeed, there have been situations and times in my life when my blindness has caused me to feel inadequate, fearful or left out. These feelings occur most often when I have been faced with disappointment or a new and uncomfortable situation.

My blindness has caused me to learn to do most everything differently from a sighted person - reading, writing, cooking, traveling, telling time, shopping, watching TV. Most important of all, it affects how, when and if I acquire information for my personal and professional needs. I rely on family, friends, readers, strangers, my computer, braille, radio and television, my inquisitive nature and deductive reasoning to piece together the information that I require.

I can't honestly say how blindness has affected my life-style, because I don't know how or if my life-style would have been different from what it has been. I've been very fortunate to be able to pursue three different careers and live in two countries through my own choice.

The limitation of blindness that has most annoyed me has to do with travel. In my job as an HR manager with a Fortune 500 company, I traveled regularly by air, bus and automobile throughout a five-state area. To do this effectively required careful advance planning and relying on help and cooperation from airline and hotel personnel, skycaps, fellow travelers and colleagues. Not being able to drive a car has meant a lot of pre-planning for doctor and dental appointments, business meetings and social activities. Last minute schedule changes can be really vexing.

I struggle most with what psychologists would call the social tendency characterized as "passivity and dependency." At times, I have resented having to rely on my wife and children to read things to me, to address an envelope, to take me somewhere, and so forth. They are busy and have their own priorities. I used to bully them; now I negotiate with them or find another way. Also, I have come to realize that we all depend on each other, even though sighted people may not see it that way.

I have encountered the full range of stereotypical negative attitudes toward blindness throughout my life. Even in recent years, and despite my significant educational, vocational and personal accomplishments, I am indulged, excused, pitied, shunned, admired, rejected, sympathized with, envied, patronized, and discriminated against. This happens even with supposedly intelligent, informed and enlightened adults.

It affects me in two ways: my personal self-perception and my opportunities to perform a task. I have more control over the former than the latter. If I am thought incapable of performing a particular task because of my blindness, it is often very difficult to convince people to give me the opportunity to try.

It is not easy to prevent this prejudgment from happening, and try to explain or demonstrate to those willing to see and understand what I am capable of doing. I also conduct workshops, give public talks and write articles to explode the myths and misperceptions that people have toward persons with disabilities.

There are various types of relationships that impact, to a greater or lesser degree, on a visually impaired individual's self-esteem. Among these are: the non-person or impersonal relationship and those relationships based on common stereotypes. Time and experience have taught me to balance and moderate their impact. Occasionally, I have chosen to have some fun with them.

Not long ago I was in a restaurant with a friend of mine. The waiter came up to the table and asked my friend: "What does he (referring to me) want to eat?" My friend is deaf but speaks quite well. So, using sign language, I interpreted the question for him and then told him what to order for me. He told the waiter what I wanted. Then the waiter asked him: "And what would you like sir?" I signed the question to my friend who signed his answer back to me, and I told the now thoroughly bewildered waiter what my friend wanted to order. We had a good laugh.

The point that we wanted to get across to the waiter was that whether you are speaking to a blind person, a deaf person, or a person in a wheelchair, speak to that person and not to them through a third party. I think he got the message.

I don't always win these educational encounters, however. Here is another example of a personal encounter based on stereotypical attitudes that left me frustrated and dissatisfied.

At the airport a man came up to me and, noticing that I was wearing a business suit and tie he said: "I'll bet you're a computer programmer. I have a friend who's blind, and he's a fantastic programmer."

"Well, no, actually I'm not." I replied.

"But you do use a computer," he insisted.

"Well, yes, to some degree," I admitted.

"I knew it," he said. "Blind people are good with computers." And with that, he hurried away. Thus was his stereotype of the kind of job that a blind person in today's world can do.

There's another type of relationship and attitude that causes me more amusement than annoyance. Well-intentioned friends and colleagues will comment: "You know, I sometimes forget you're blind." This is supposed to be a compliment. But I truly don't want them to forget that I'm blind. This "forgetting" has caused these same friends to leave me standing in the parking lot as they headed off toward the entrance to the restaurant.

There is another relationship or attitude that can be most destructive and debilitating to a blind individual's self-esteem. It is to be the object of pity and regret. To be pitied is to be devalued and humiliated. I am quite vocally intolerant of this type of relationship and attitude.

My mother, who had no formal training or counseling in raising a blind child, was amazingly intuitive in knowing how to bring the world to my fingertips, show me things by touch. To the circus clown, the storekeeper, the policeman on his motorcycle, the fire chief, the milkman with his horse-drawn wagon - she would declare: "He has to touch to see what it is." This approach and attitude have stood me in good stead all my life and have been a positive influence on my way of seeing the world. I thank her for this in my prayers every day.

I am fortunate to have numerous relationships based on respect and friendship with professional colleagues, my family and a wide circle of personal acquaintances.

There are essentially two standards of performance that we use in judging our success or failure in life. The "community" standard or social comparison for judging one's performance is based on the expectations (aspirations) and priority values of society, family and friends. These expectations can become self-fulfilling prophecies and directly affect, negatively or positively, the academic achievements of students and the rehabilitative potential of visually-impaired adults.

The other is the "personal" standard and is based upon proof of worth to oneself.

With the former, the individual strives for approval of others. With the latter, the individual seeks to become competent, productive and responsible and, in so doing, demonstrate to himself/herself proof of self-worth.

Judgments of failure by an individual may result in one of four possible responses: 1. Try harder/find another way; 2. Change your aspirations or goals; 3. Lower your standards, that is, be content with less; or 4. Give up. Repeated failures build patterns for future failures and for striving less and giving up more quickly.

Adjusting to blindness is part of the normal process of accommodating to life's many traumas and crises. Adjustment is a dynamic, on-going process that continues throughout life. Adjusting to blindness is adjusting to life with the added stress of blindness.

There are three principle changes that must take place in a person's attitude and values during the adjustment process:

- A receding of our feelings of self-pity and anger as we begin the process of examining and reconsidering the meaning of life - our basic assumptions, values, beliefs, priorities and habitual patterns of behavior.

- A beginning toward the acceptance of blindness as a fact and as one of our personal attributes, "a condition of life." This also becomes, for the individual, part of our discovering our new identity.

- The setting of new goals, a searching for solutions and alternatives. It also marks the start of being willing to modify or change how goals can be met, based on a realistic understanding of one's strengths and limitations.

Common characteristics of a person who is having difficulty adjusting to his/her visual impairment are:

Exhibits apathy, withdrawal and isolation;

Has low expectations and a poor image of all other blind persons;

Maintains an unrealistic hope for restoration of sight; and

Exhibits anger and escape into drugs, alcohol and other destructive social behavior. I have personally witnessed this in blind persons I have known.

By contrast, characteristics which typify a person who is doing better adjusting to his/her visual impairment are:

Prefers independence and tends to be self-directed;

Uses adaptive aids and techniques without reservation;

Has a healthy self-acceptance and self-respect; and

Enjoys and participates in recreational activities.

A person must love self and accept self, before he or she can love and accept another. If I don't like me, I don't see how anyone else could like me either. If I am so focused on what an awful person I must be, that there is no room in my thoughts to see the good in you. I am truly blind, deaf and closed-minded to the good in me and the good in you.

These concepts are presented in greater detail in the excellent book "Self-esteem and Adjusting with Blindness," by Dean W. Tuttle and Naomi R. Tuttle, published by

Charles C. Thomas, Springfield, IL, 1996.

My age has provided me with many years of experience in discovering a wide array of techniques and approaches to deal with those problems occasioned by blindness. My concerns today are more for my children and grandchildren. In recent years I have experienced a mild hearing loss which has raised in my mind the specter of how I might deal with a second disability.

I have only slight light perception in my right eye. It does not fluctuate from place to place or time to time and has remained stable for more than 40 years. This constancy has helped me to focus on developing adaptive skills and techniques.

The computer, with speech and braille output, has been a tremendous aid to me both in my work and in my personal life. I also use a scanner and an Optacon to read printed material, a braille embosser and Perkins braille writer, to produce documents in readable format, and a braille Note laptop computer for taking notes at meetings. I work with MS Word, Excel, Windows Explorer, Outlook Express, OpenBook, Duxbury and JAWS. Notwithstanding all of this, I still have need of sighted assistance for information access. Although I can read a great deal of print material with a scanner, some correspondence still comes to me hand-written or of poor print quality requiring my reliance on a sighted person to read it.

I confess that I am the eternal optimist, which I undoubtedly owe to my mother. Her philosophy was, "*Always do the best you can. Don't waste* time feeling sorry for yourself or anger toward someone else. *Life is too short*."

Although my mother had never previously known anyone who was blind, she decided that she was going to make every effort to see that I had as normal a life as possible. She went to great lengths in order that I might have the same opportunities as my sighted brother and sisters - opportunities to learn to dance, to swim, to ride a horse, to ice skate, to play baseball - opportunities to go to the movies, to concerts, to the zoo, to the amusement park. Whatever it was that my brother and sisters did or wanted to do, she looked for a way for me to take part as well. She recognized that although I might not be able to do some things in the same manner as my sighted siblings, it was nevertheless important that I have the chance to try.

Her philosophy became my philosophy, and I have tried to pass it along to my six children and 20 grandchildren.

I can't really separate my attitude toward life as a visually-impaired person from my basic outlook on life. They are the same. Life is full of adversity, but it is also full of adventure and opportunity and wonder. My blindness is part of me like my tallness, my big feet and my liking for black licorice. I care about people more than I care about things, and I try to live each day with joy by giving joy and hope and love to others.

People who lose their sight late in life possess a rich storehouse of memories of having seen. This allows them to "visualize" situations, people, objects and scenes. They can borrow from their memory bank to construct mental pictures of images described to them by others. They understand and more easily can communicate feelings and thoughts via facial expressions and gestures. On the downside, their personal, vocational and social adjustment to a visual loss is generally more difficult. This difficulty increases as the onset of visual loss comes later in life. Learning new skills (for working, walking, reading, writing, cooking, etc.) is harder as one gets older.

A person born with a visual impairment is taught coping skills at a very early age. Learning to use special aides, adaptive technology and more effective and efficient use of other senses comes more easily and naturally to young children. If the child is born with no vision at all, there is a definite challenge for him/her to learn and appreciate the concept of color, spatial movement and expressive body language.

There is, of course, the whole question of how much vision loss the person experiences. Many people who are considered "legally blind" do retain some vision. The degree to which they can see and how they use this vision will be an important determinant in their level of personal and social independence. Check the American

Foundation for the Blind website www.afb.org for more information on this topic.

A final note. Yes, Blindness has its limitations, its inconveniences, and its moments of frustration, but what I can assure you is there is life after loss of sight. I urge you to remember, whether you're dealing with a client, colleague, family member or friend who is visually impaired, always look at the person behind the disability, not just at the disability.

(Note: Some of the concepts relating to adjusting to blindness, referred to in this Foreward, are from the excellent book "Self-esteem and Adjusting with Blindness," and are used with permission of the authors, Dean W. Tuttle and Naomi R. Tuttle, published by Charles C. Thomas, Springfield, IL, 1996.)

MESSAGE FROM JIMMY

I was always proud of you, "Big Little Brother," for what you accomplished throughout your life, and that would hold true whether you were sighted or not. Still do.

I guess as a kid I just accepted the way you were, and never thought much about it. I just thought of you as a normal kid, kind of bright, but who couldn't see. We played quite a bit together when we were very young, and relied a lot on our imaginations unlike kids do today. There was radio, which we listened to a lot, and from listening to radio we were inspired to create our own stories. We took the roles of various characters, and being the older brother, I liked being the dominant character. These characters were various animals that talked and acted like humans. We even used your tape recorder to record our own radio skits.

I have been thinking more and more these days about just how precious life really is. Unfortunately, it seems to take a crisis in our lives to come to this realization. I have so many things to be thankful for...and not the least of which has been a brother

like you. You know, I have looked up to you for a long time, and not just because you're taller than I.
    Love, LBB (Little Big Brother), Jim

INSIDE MY WORLD

By Larry P. Johnson

Yes, not being able to see does present some problems. I remember once standing on a street corner in Chicago waiting for a bus and wanting to know if I was at the right corner. Just then I heard a footstep a few feet away. I turned and asked, "Pardon me, does the Montrose Avenue bus stop here?"

Getting no answer, I tried again, a little louder. Still no answer. I was sure I had heard someone. So, I raised my voice even louder and said with a touch of annoyance, "Excuse me. Are you a sir or a madam?"

The answer I got was: Pwrrr! I had been speaking to a milk wagon horse.

My mom used to say to people about me: "He's in his own little world." I wasn't sure what she meant by that. Was it because I was blind that she thought my perception and understanding of the world was so different from that of a sighted person? Perhaps. Certainly it is true that seeing the world without sight is seeing it in a very different way. The reach of our other senses -- our hearing, touch and smell -- is much shorter than the reach of our ability to see. In that respect, the world of a blind person is indeed much smaller, much closer and much more limited.

Perhaps she thought that my being blind meant that I spent more time living in a fantasy world created by my own imagination. Yes, it is true that freed of the constant distraction of visual images occasioned by one's surroundings, a blind person may more readily turn their thoughts inward and entertain themselves with daydreams of the past or fantasies about the future. Yet, at the same time, I would argue that it allows for easier concentration and deeper reflection on problems, plans and possibilities.

It used to bother me a lot when Mom would make that statement, "He's in his own little world", to one of her friends or to a perfect stranger. But now I recognize that she was right. In fact, each of us is "in our own little world," our own personal reality. This reality is shaped not just by our senses, but by our upbringing, our education, our culture, our geography, our exposure to the environment, our interaction with people, our whole range of personal experience and learning. And so, each of us, has shaped and continues to shape a very unique personal reality, which is our world.

Through this book, I hope to give you a glimpse inside my world, in particular, my world as a blind child growing up in Chicago some 70 plus years ago.

EARLY MEMORIES

M y earliest memory of being blind was wearing a pair of dark glasses, painted black with shoe polish, and a stocking cap pulled down over my nose. My enemy was light. Direct light from the sun or a lamp caused me excruciating pain.

At six months of age I was diagnosed with congenital glaucoma, a disease in which fluid builds up behind the eyeball producing pressure on the optic nerve, eventually killing it. In most cases of glaucoma, there is no pain or warning. In my case, however, there were both.

Shortly after I was born, our family moved to Baltimore Maryland, my father being transferred there by the company he worked for. My parents consulted with doctors at Johns Hopkins University Hospital, then and now one of the finest medical facilities in the country, about my eye condition. I had three operations, incisions on my eyeballs to drain off the fluid and release the pressure. However, this gave only temporary relief. Once the incisions closed and the fluid built up again, the pressure and the pain returned.

Larry at age 5 sitting on front steps
of house in Baltimore.

My vision did not go all at once. I remember, at age four, being able to distinguish between a fork and spoon held a few inches in front of my face. I could also identify colors. However, I had to do it in twilight. I could not bear the pain of opening my eyes in direct light. Gradually my vision worsened, and I was able to put aside the stocking cap but continued to wear the dark glasses. By age nine, my vision had deteriorated to the point to where I no longer needed to wear the dark glasses either.

I can only imagine the anguish and frustration my parents must have felt about having a blind child. They had no prior experience with blindness or with blind people. None of my siblings or relatives on either side of the family had serious vision problems. For some people fear of blindness is worse than the fear of death. I learned many years later that my favorite aunt, my Aunt Mildred, had divorced my Uncle Joe in part because she was afraid that my blindness might be hereditary, and she just couldn't face the prospect of bearing a blind child.

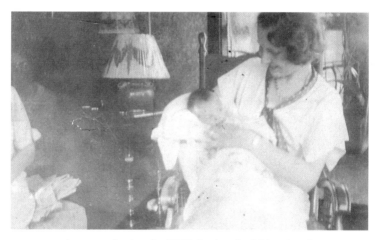

Larry as baby, in 1933, being held by Aunt
Mildred Johnson at the house on Kenton, with
Grandma Johnson barely visible in background.

Sighted people worry a lot about blind people falling over things, breaking things, spilling things, and burning holes in the carpet. And, they worry about what they would do if they became blind.

Blind people worry about being stared at, being pitied, about burning holes in the carpet, falling over things, breaking or spilling things and about being accepted by the sighted world.

Mom had seven children in ten years, three of whom did not survive. I was her last. She married late, at age 28. She was 39 when I was born. Did her age contribute in any way to my infirmity? Probably not. Glaucoma in infants is relatively rare, and the cause is still not very well understood.

When I was six, my parents separated. The reason was my father's weakness for playing the horses. He was introduced to the thrill and addiction of racetrack betting by his co-workers several years before I was born. At first, it was for him only an occasional vice, but gradually and inevitably the addiction grew. He was a brilliant accountant and earned a very good salary. He was so good with numbers that he genuinely believed that he could "beat the ponies." He would tell our mom that he was sure that with the next race, the next bet, his pick would win, and we'd be on easy street. He began pawning our furniture, even our refrigerator, whatever he could, to get money to place one more bet.

His boss tried to help by transferring him back to the company's Chicago office, but Dad couldn't stay away from the racetrack. Things got so bad financially that we were forced to move in with our paternal grandmother, her invalid daughter, Aunt

Helen and her other son, Uncle Joe. They lived in a beautiful two-story brick home on Kenton Avenue, on Chicago's northwest side. We lived there for a little over a year.

Picture of Dad in grandma Johnson's backyard, around 1939. Part of a garage is in the background. He is in a crouched position, wearing a white shirt and tie.

Uncle Joe loved baseball and was a staunch Chicago White Sox fan, even though they were the team that played on the Southside and were always in last place. All of us kids became rabid Sox fans too. I remain loyal to the pale hose even though it has been more than 50 years since I lived in Chicago. It took 85 years for the Sox to finally win another World Series.

Saturdays and Sundays during the baseball season, Uncle Joe would have the big radio in the living room tuned to the Sox game. That radio, which was taller than I, had a huge speaker. I was in awe of it, even a little frightened by it. I was certain that the people who spoke on the radio were somehow actually inside of that big brown box. Of course, I didn't know then that one day I would be joining them.

Once Uncle Joe drove us to Des Moines Iowa to visit my mom's brother and sister--Aunt Marie and Uncle Fritz. We drove at night, sleeping most of the way. I remember waking up as we were crossing the Mississippi River. It felt so scary driving over that big, wide bridge. I thought, *what if it should fall down into the river, with us on it*? I didn't know how to swim. Thank heavens it didn't.

Grandma's house had a huge beautiful brick fireplace, made with bricks brought all the way from Wisconsin. There were four large bedrooms upstairs. In the basement, Uncle Joe had a couple of slot machines, that really worked, and a

Victrola that played 78 rpm. Records—records by Enrico Caruso and Guy Lombardo.

Next to the kitchen was a huge pantry stocked with lots of Grandma's home-made pickles and preserves--plum, apricot, tomato and crabapple jelly; the latter made from crabapples picked from a tall tree in the backyard.

Grandma was from Germany and a wonderful cook. I remember her delicious cinnamon coffee cakes and apple kuchen. At Christmas, she baked her special anise cookies, minced meat pies and fruit cakes. What glorious smells her oven produced. It was so hard waiting for dessert after dinner!

Seated at the dinner table, we were commanded by Uncle Joe to eat everything that was served us. I can still hear him saying "Mop your plate." And he meant it, literally. With a piece of bread you were supposed to sop up every last little bit of gravy and not leave a single carrot or pea or string bean. "Remember the poor starving people over in Europe," he would say. I used to think, *how can my eating my carrots help the poor starving people over in Europe? Why don't we get a box and I'll put all my carrots in it and we can send it to them.* Funny isn't it, what adults say to kids to get them to eat their veggies?

The house on Kenton Avenue was just a couple of blocks from the St. Paul train tracks. Lying in bed at night, I'd listen to the quickening chug, chug,

chug--chugchugchugchug of those mighty loco-
motives and the melancholy wail of their steam
whistles. I'd wonder to what far-away places they
would be going. I thought how exciting it would
be to climb on board one of those magnificent
trains and travel far, far away to some distant city.
It would be a dozen years later that I would board
a train in Chicago and travel by rail for three days
with my guide dog, Tasha, all the way to Mexico
City.

During the day, we kids would sometimes walk
to the viaduct, climb up on to the train trestle and,
to show just how brave we were, stand less than
ten feet from the track to watch one of the express
passenger trains speed by. The engineer would
shoot off some steam and blow his whistle just as
he passed, which scared the daylights out of us.

We lived with Grandma, Uncle Joe and Aunt
Helen for a little over a year. Grandma Elizabeth
Johnson was 81 when she died in 1942.

I remember going to her funeral. I was nine.
Mom had me touch the casket just before they
lowered it into the ground. It made an awful im-
pression on me, just thinking about Grandma being put in that deep hole and covered up with
dirt. *What if she were to wake up*, my little mind
asked. Since then, I've never liked going to funerals. And, maybe partly because of this childhood
experience, I've decided I don't want to be buried

when I die, but cremated instead. I want to take no chances of being buried alive.

A SINGLE MOM

My mom had amazing fortitude and courage. Only now, as a parent and grandparent reflecting back upon my own struggles and those of my children, can I truly appreciate and admire her for her strength of character and commitment to independence.

When she realized that Dad just could not or would not conquer his addiction to gambling, she decided to separate from him. Although she had only a high school education and no work experience, she resolved to take her four children and make it on her own. She sold her beautiful dining-room table, the last possession of value she owned and used the money to rent the first floor of a two-story frame farmhouse at 5653 W. Montrose Avenue, on Chicago's far northwest side, about a mile and a half from the city limits. The rent was $20 a month.

The wood frame house sat alone on the block, with wide open prairie on either side and across the street. And so it was fully exposed to the elements. This became frigidly clear during the long cold winters we lived there. Our house had two bedrooms, a living-room, dining-room, kitchen and a laundry room. My sisters, Dorothy and

Eileen, shared one of the bedrooms. My brother, Jimmy, slept on a day bed in the dining room, and I slept with my mom in the other bedroom. I didn't mind it at first, when I was six. But as I got older, 10 and 11, I became embarrassed about it and didn't want people to know that I slept with my mom.

Our mother believed firmly in the healthful benefits of fresh air, even in the dead of winter. She'd open our bedroom window an inch or so in order to, as she put it, "let in some clean, fresh air." It really did smell clean and fresh, and even now I can enjoy small doses of crisp, cold winter weather. To keep warm, she would have me put on a pair of heavy flannel pajamas and thick winter socks. I'd crawl under three layers of blankets and sheets and cover my head with a wool sweater, towel or second pillow. All that would be exposed would be my nose. (That habit has remained with me. Even now, on cool evenings, I like to sleep with my head buried under a pillow. It gives my kids a chuckle to see me covered up with my head buried like an ostrich.)

The heating for our home was provided by a coal stove that sat at one end of the dining-room, just outside Mom's and my bedroom. My brother, Jimmy, and sister, Eileen, were responsible for hauling the coal in a bucket from the coal bin in the laundry room to the stove. During the winter, to save on fuel, the stove would be dampered down at night, and both bedroom doors would be kept closed. In the morning, we'd jump out of bed, grab our clothes and dash to the stove to dress, pushing and shoving to be as close as possible to the warmth. Sometimes, when it was really cold, Mom would light the gas oven in the kitchen, and some of us would huddle next to it as we quickly dressed. There was no dilly-dallying around getting dressed when the temperature in the house was just barely above freezing.

The summers in Chicago were hot and humid. Having no air-conditioning and only one electric fan, we opened the windows and hoped for an easterly breeze off Lake Michigan. Many nights there was none. On those evenings, sleep was difficult as sweat-soaked pillows were turned four and five times during the night, and mosquitoes hungrily hummed and whirled about our heads. I'd lie awake, exposing just enough flesh to entice one of the little bloodsuckers to land on my arm, forehead or cheek and then slap myself fast and hard, hoping to feel a crushed little insect body beneath my hand. Other times, I'd play the coward and hide myself under the sheets to avoid being a meal.

At first, Mom paid the bills by working as a "cleaning lady" for other women who worked in offices and factories. She scrubbed floors, vacuumed rugs, made beds, washed and ironed clothes, and babysat sick children. On days when I stayed home from school because of a cold or sore throat, she would take me along to her job, give me some modeling clay or a few toy soldiers or cars to play with, sit me in a corner and go about her chores.

Doing domestic work had to be particularly hard and humbling for our mom. She was born of upper middleclass German immigrant parents and was raised in an atmosphere of comfort and abundance. Yet, her strong sense of pride and personal stubbornness prevented her from asking for help from relatives or accepting welfare. She resolved to work at whatever she could to earn money to pay the rent and buy food and clothing for her children. Although our suppers often featured the same simple menu of ground round steak, boiled potatoes and a vegetable, we never went hungry or without warm clothes to wear. At one point, she worked as a cashier at Riverview, the local amusement park. Later, she got a job as an elevator operator at a swank apartment house on Lake Shore Drive. Still later, she taught herself to type and got jobs as office receptionist and office manager. Mom continually sought ways to improve herself for the benefit of her family, and she taught us to do the same. Both of my sisters, Dorothy and Eileen, helped contribute to the family income by doing baby-sitting on weekends when they were just 12 years old. And my brother

Jim, when he was old enough, sold popcorn and peanuts at the nearby girls' softball stadium.

VICTORY GARDEN

L ike many other American families during the war years in the early 1940's, we had a victory garden. The open prairie next to our house was perfect--rich and fertile, and no one objected to our using it to plant a few vegetables. We raised corn, radishes, carrots, tomatoes, cucumbers, onions, green beans, peas and potatoes. Mom had me help with the planting, watering and pulling of weeds. At harvest time it became a wonderful source of additional food for our table. I was always eager to sample the crunchy red radishes and crispy orange carrots freshly pulled from the ground. Because our garden was pesticide-free, there was no need to wash the vegetables, just brush away the excess dirt before popping them into your mouth. Sooo good!

We also had a rhubarb patch that grew wild along the east wall of the house that Mom regularly harvested, then cooked and baked into delicious rhubarb pies. Yes, despite Mom working many long, hard hours each day, she somehow found time to keep her own house clean, wash, iron and sew our clothes, mend socks, cook and bake fruit pies, oatmeal cookies and cinnamon coffeecake. Yum, how I loved those coffeecakes with the thick, crunchy chunks of cinnamon and sugar on top. They were so tempting that I would sneak up to the kitchen counter where they were cooling, peel off a piece of cinnamon topping and slip it into my mouth. Of course, I wasn't the only culprit. My brother and sisters loved coffeecakes just as much as I did. And so, by the time mealtime came around, when Mom planned to serve the coffeecake, mysteriously half the topping was already eaten. She fussed at us a little but was understanding and forgave our impatience.

Fruit cakes were always a favorite holiday tradition in our house, and Mom made them from scratch. Even now, for me Christmas is not complete unless I can get my hands on a couple of fruit cakes. Unfortunately, I now have to settle for store bought, but I still love those morsels of candied citrus and nuts, washed down with a tall glass of ice cold milk.

SCHOOL DAYS

When I was six, Mom and I took a long train ride from Chicago to Jacksonville Illinois, where the state residential school for the blind is located. She was considering enrolling me there. She told them about my need to wear dark glasses and the stocking cap because the light hurt my eyes. They recommended removal of both my eyes and replacing them with artificial ones.

They said this would solve the problem of my experiencing pain from being exposed to light and would also improve my appearance aesthetically, because I would no longer need the glasses or stocking cap. Mom hesitated. She understood the logic of their suggestion. But at the same time, she didn't want to deprive me of what useful vision might remain once the glaucoma condition stabilized. In the end, she chose not to follow their advice, and we took the train back to Chicago. I'm glad she made that decision.

Still searching for answers, she took me to see a specialist at the Illinois Eye, Ear, Nose and Throat hospital in Chicago. The doctor insisted on forcing my eyes open and shining a flashlight directly at them. The pain was terrible. I screamed and kicked trying to get away. He, too, recommended removing my eyes and replacing them with artificial ones. Mom resisted.

Shortly thereafter, she learned that the Chicago Board of Education had established an innovative program for mainstreaming blind children into the public school system, and she decided to enroll me in it. Of course, they didn't call it "mainstreaming" back then.

There continues to be a major debate among parents, educators and students as to the comparative advantages and disadvantages of a specialized residential school for blind children versus a "mainstreamed" integrated public school setting for the education of children who are visually impaired. I believe both have a role to play and should be available as alternative CHOICES to be considered and evaluated by parents.

And so it was that I began attending Burley Grammar School on Chicago's near north side. From kindergarten through the fourth grade, all of my classes were taken in a self-contained classroom with Miss Baker. Although she was fully sighted, Miss Baker could both read and write braille fluently and expected that every one of her students should likewise become proficient in braille. She gave us homework in braille every night. Oh how I hated it then, but I am truly grateful to her today. I have used braille throughout college, in every one of my jobs and daily in my personal life. I use it to keep tract of telephone numbers, to take notes at meetings, keep my checking account balanced, label audio and video cassettes, floppy disks, personal papers, office file folders, credit cards, clothing tags, checks, business cards, playing cards, spices and condiments in the kitchen, the microwave oven, and a great deal more. The convenience of braille is that it can be read in the dark, without electricity or batteries. It can also be read on the beach, while riding on a bus, waiting in the dentist's office, or singing with the church choir. I believe braille improves one's literacy and should be taught to every blind child.

Miss Baker kept a large bottle of lilac water in a cabinet next to her desk. She insisted on rewarding her students, boys and girls alike, who did well on their braille and other assignments, with a large dose of lilac water on our collars or lapels. It made me feel like such a sissy. To this day, whenever I smell lilacs I am reminded of those embarrassing perfumed baptisms from Miss Baker.

Miss Baker had another bottle that she kept in her desk drawer. From time to time she would take it out and swig down a couple of swallows. She told us it was her cough medicine, but it sure smelled a lot like my Uncle Joe's Kentucky bourbon. One thing for sure, she never offered to share it with us.

The week before Christmas vacation at school was a no-study week. Miss Baker gave us sheets of colored paper which we cut into 3 by 1 inch strips, curled and pasted into circles, and then linked them together in long chains. It was fun getting the gooey paste all over our desks, our hands and arms, our faces and in our hair. The competition was to see who could make the longest chain.

We put on a short Christmas play when I was in second and third grade, a reenactment of the birth of Jesus, with wise men and shepherds and the Holy family. The older kids got the speaking roles. I was a shepherd, which meant I just stood quietly in the background in my shepherd's costume. It was my first on-stage appearance.

19

Back then, it was politically correct to perform religious plays and sing Christmas carols in school. One of Miss Baker's former students, a man named Bill, would visit her class during the week before Christmas and play Christmas songs on the piano for us to sing along. He knew them all. Bill was kind of strange, in that he talked very slowly, and when he played, he moved his head back and forth in time with the music. I've heard that a lot of blind musicians do this. I've always wondered why. I don't remember moving my head around when I played the piano or accordion. Am I the odd one?

Besides emphasizing the importance of knowing braille, Miss Baker stressed the need for us to train our memories. She had us memorize and recite numerous classic poems like The Midnight Ride of Paul Revere and famous speeches, like Lincoln's Gettysburg Address, fragments of which, incredibly, I can still remember to this day. Miss Baker knew that developing a good memory would be a big asset for us in school and later in life; again, she was right.

George, the son of a Presbyterian minister, was one of my classmates in Miss Baker's room. He was very studious and extremely smart. We would compete to see who could memorize the fastest whatever poem or speech Miss Baker might happen to give us. Once we learned our assignment, Miss Baker would take us around to other classrooms so that we could show off in front of the sighted students.

George and I were in the fifth grade when his older brother, Albert, came across an elaborately complex and obscure medical definition of a common physical phenomenon. He dictated it to George and me and then challenged us to memorize it. Well, we did. And then we made it a game to see who could say it the fastest. Here is how I remember it went:

"A temporary erythema and calorific effulgence of the physiognomy, ocliogized by the perceptiveness of the sensorium, when a predicament of inequitability resulting from a sense of shame, anger or other causes, eventuated in the pareses of the vasomotor filaments of the facial capillaries whereby being divested of their natural elasticity are suffused with a radiant irradiated compound circulating nutrient liquid emanating from the animated pericardium." (Excerpted from the Foolish Dictionary by Gideaon Wurdz)

What did I say? It is the definition of a blush.

One day George brought a little mud turtle to school for me. He left it in a milk carton in the cloak room. Somehow it got out and started crawling around the room. Miss Baker saw it and screamed. She let us know in no uncertain terms that we'd better "get that animal out of the room and never let it come back."

Well, I took it home and kept it as a pet for about a year until it escaped. Five years later, my brother found it in the rhubarb patch next to the house. It had quadrupled in size. Since it apparently had done very well on its own, I decided to let it keep its liberty.

During those years in grammar school, we brought our lunch to school each day. There was no cafeteria or snack machines. The milk-man came each day to deliver little 6-oz. bottles of milk, that cost just a penny. Mom would make me two half sandwiches -- peanut butter and jelly, liver sausage (That's what we called it, but I have since learned that the correct name is liver worst.) bologna or cheese -- wrapped in wax paper, a banana or orange and always a few cookies for dessert. Some of the kids brought Polish sausage or salami sandwiches. Wow, the odor of garlic was overpowering. I've since learned that the best way to counteract the smell of garlic on someone else's breath is to eat plenty of garlic yourself.

It was when we were in the fifth grade that our class of blind kids was transferred to Alexander Graham Bell, a much larger and newer elementary school. That's when our "mainstreaming" (integration with sighted students) began. First one class, then another, gradually adding more each semester until, by the eighth grade, all of our classes were integrated with sighted students. It was in fifth grade that we also learned to type, so that we could prepare our assignments and turn in examinations to the sighted teachers who didn't know braille.

We went back to our homeroom to study, practice our typing and braille skills and complete our assignments. In our homeroom we had braille writers, typewriters, arithmetic boards, braille dictionaries, braille reference books, a world globe in relief, and several wooden maps that could be taken apart and put back together like a jigsaw puzzle. Holding those pieces in my hands, it gave me a real feel for the shape and relative size of the individual states of our United States and that of other countries.

THE LAUNDRY ROOM

I hate flies and I hate mosquitoes. I hate mosquitoes because they suck your blood. I hate flies because they are annoying. They land on your nose. They land on your food. So, whenever I have a chance to squash a fly, I will. Our house on Montrose had a laundry room and, in the summer, a few flies would always sneak in there. Now flies in a dark laundry room will always gather near the window. One hot August day, I decided to declare war on the fly population. I searched for and found the fly spray gun in the kitchen and quietly crept to the laundry room. I could hear the buzzing flies by the window. There must have been five or six of the devils. I took aim and sprayed, and sprayed, and sprayed, and sprayed. The buzzing subsided. I smiled with satisfaction. All dead. Just then Mom came in.

"What on earth are you doing?" She asked.

"Killing flies." I announced triumphantly.

"Well, you've also managed to kill three of my ferns which were there on the windowsill."

Alas, every war has its casualties.

What is it about fire that fascinates? When I was eight, (maybe I was nine), I almost set our house on fire. My brother Jimmy and I would sometimes go out into the prairie away from the house, build a camp fire and roast potatoes. We would roll the potatoes into the hot ashes after the fire had died down, and then wait until the outer skin was completely black. Then we'd roll them back out, split them open with a sharp knife, shake some salt on to them and scoop out the steaming insides. They smelled and tasted incredibly good. If really hungry, we'd chew on the crunchy charcoal shell.

Fire was our friend. It cooked our food, gave us warmth, and cleared the prairie of weeds when we wanted to play baseball. It obeyed our commands.

I still had enough vision then that I could see light and shadow and distinguish bright colors. I could see fire, its red embers, yellow flames and white smoke. I was confident that I could control it. One afternoon, I was playing by myself in the laundry room. It was a little chilly. I thought, a little fire would be very nice. The floor of the laundry room was cement, so I felt it would be safe to stack a few newspapers on the floor and light them. I would make just a little fire, just to take the chill out. I went into the kitchen and found the box of wooden matches Mom always kept there. I crumpled up a bunch of newspapers, placing them right in the center of the laundry room and struck the match. The paper caught fire right away. How pretty it looked. How nice and warm it felt. The flames got higher and higher. Wow! It's a pretty big fire, I thought.

Just then the door opened and my mother appeared. "What in the Sam Hill are you doing?"

"Just making a little fire," I murmured.

"Get inside!" She commanded. I obeyed. Fortunately for me, the washtubs in the laundry room were filled with water, and Mom scooped out a quick bucketful of water and doused out my campfire, averting disaster. I deserved and received a good whipping that day and promised that all future campfires would be outside.

GAMES WE PLAYED

The games we played in elementary school were pretty much the same games that sighted kids played – London Bridge, Ring-around-the-rosy, "May I?" and musical chairs. This was my favorite. We'd line up the chairs, one less than the number of players, facing them alternately one to the left and one to the right. Miss Baker would put a record on the old phonograph and we'd start marching around the row of chairs. Suddenly the music would stop, and everyone would scramble to get in a chair. Of course, one person would be left without a chair, and they'd be out. Then we'd remove a chair, and the music would start again. Finally, it would get down to just two people and one chair. I'd usually manage to be one of the last two. My technique for winning was to keep a hand on the back of the remaining chair at all times. When the music stopped, if I happened to be on the wrong side of the chair, I'd grab hold of the back of the chair and flip it around. This resulted in my opponent losing his balance and falling on the floor while I plunked myself down in the chair and was declared the winner. Sometimes though my opponent would have the same idea, and we'd wind up both sitting in the chair or both on the floor.

At home Jimmy, Dorothy, Eileen, their friends and I would sometimes play outdoor games like tag, hide-and-seek or baseball. Mom always made sure that they included me in. "Let your brother play too" she'd say.

In the laundry room, with all the lights turned out, we played a scary murder game where we drew cards to see who was to be the victim and who was to be the murderer. Then, a third person, the police detective, was to question all the witnesses and try to solve the crime.

On rainy days, we might stay indoors and play monopoly, Chinese checkers or pinochle, our favorite card game.

Since there was no TV, no game boards, no Ipods, we had to create our own entertainment. Jimmy and I created adventure stories involving two amazing cats called the Friskies and a dog named Skippy. Our imagined heroes got into all sorts of dangerous situations involving criminals and assorted bad guys. Our adventure stories could last for hours or even days. But, in the end, good triumphed over evil, and the Friskies and Skippy emerged unscathed.

TWO SISTERS

I had two beautiful sisters. (The younger, Eileen, passed away a few years ago.) Dorothy is the oldest, and 6 years older than I. When we were kids we used to call her Dot. I don't think she much liked the nickname, and as we got older, we began using her full name. A tall, 5 ft. 9 inch, striking blonde, Dorothy has always been a kind of second mother to Jimmy and me, and she still is. She is the one who remembers birthdays and reminds us to call our other siblings. When I was just 19, because our dad was out of the picture and Jimmy was away in the Army, I had the special thrill and honor of giving Dorothy away at her wedding. Wow! I felt really grown-up and important.

Larry, in 1955, walking sister Dorothy down the aisle at Our Lady of Mercy Church in Chicago.

Before she got married, Dorothy used to love to host get-togethers for her friends at our house. I loved them too, because she would make a whole lot of delicious snacks to serve, and I always managed to get my share. Particularly popular with her friends, and with me, were her very creative molds of multilayered, multicolored Jell-O.

Eileen, we called her Leen, (and she was, slender like our mom) was born in Baltimore as Jimmy was. Dorothy and I were born in Chicago. Eileen was a brunette, like Mom and me. Jimmy and Dorothy are the blondes. Eileen was also quite tall, 5 ft. 7 inches, same as our mom. Both Dad and Uncle Joe were 6 feet, so our tall genes came from both sides of the family. Eileen married much later than Dorothy, so she was at home with me and Mom a lot longer. Eileen was quite attractive and always took great care with her appearance - using special skin creams and body lotions to keep her good complexion. Before she got married she worked at Marshall Fields as a representative for Charles of the Ritz, a very high class cosmetics company.

When I was in college, I suffered a lot from adult acne. Eileen was determined to improve my appearance by removing all the ugly blackheads on my face. She made me lie on the floor and, kneeling next to me, she used a long metal instrument with a tiny hole on the tip. Centering the tip directly over the pimpled blackhead, she pressed down hard until the pimple would pop and squirt the blackhead out. Sounds gross, I know. But Eileen took great delight and pride in popping my pimples. I meekly submitted, believing her that it would make me more attractive to girls.

In later years, like our mom, Eileen prided herself on looking 10 years younger than she was. Whenever I was with her, she would tell me to introduce her as my younger sister.

As kids, Dorothy and Eileen were really good at making candy, especially fudge and toffee. Jimmy and I helped with the toffee pulling and with the eating of both.

Popcorn was another of our favorite snacks. Our popcorn popper was a wire basket. We would put the kernels in the basket and hold it over the stove's gas flame until the first kernel popped. Then we had to lift it about an inch or two above the burner and shake it back and forth. The sound would be like setting off a hundred lady fingers on the Fourth of July. When the popping subsided, we'd open the basket and pour the fluffy popcorn into a big bowl, add melted butter and salt. It smelled soooo good and tasted even better.

SYNESTHESIA

I was about nine years old when I could finally put aside the stocking cap and dark glasses. My vision had stabilized and my eyes had become less sensitive to light. I retained light and color perception through my teen years. I still have good recall of the primary colors: blue, green, yellow, red, brown and gray. It's when people begin talking about teal, fuchsia, sepia and the like that I have difficulty understanding what they mean. But then I've learned that even my sighted friends and family aren't one hundred percent in agreement as to what these colors are. For example, I'll show a shirt or a tie to two of my daughters and get conflicting answers as to the color. Confusing? Yes.

From a very early age I have thought of letters, words, names and numbers in color. I didn't know what this condition was called until a couple of years ago. Synesthesia. It's a condition in which there's a commingling of the senses--where taste, touch, sight and sound seem to overlap. Researchers at Great Britain's Cambridge University believe that the phenomenon is experienced by perhaps only one in every two thousand persons. In my case, I see letters of the alphabet, names of people, the days of the week and the months of the year in my mind in color. My name, Larry, for example, is blue, but the letters "L" and "r" are red while "a" and "y" are black. It's not logical, makes no sense, but that's the way it comes across to me. In my mind, the alphabet is made up of 12 red letters "cfghjlqrstwx", six green letters "bdnpvz", six black letters "aeikoy" and two yellow letters "m and u". I don't think there is any practical value to it, but it's kind of fun to associate colors with words and with people's names.

It's also interesting to note that people who are synesthetes don't agree on the colors they ascribe to letters or words, and some claim that they feel textures rather than see colors.

COMING OF AGE

I made my first communion at St. Roberts's parish when I was nine. I was meek, compliant and innocent. I went to confession once a month. But it was hard coming up with sins to tell the priest so that he could give me my penance and my sins could be forgiven. I felt an obligation to exaggerate the number of my sins like lying, getting angry, not obeying my mom or fighting with my brother. It didn't occur to me that this was also lying. Still, they were only venial sins, small sins. And the penance was just a few Our Fathers and a few Hail Mary's. Later on, I had bigger sins to tell.

I was 12 when I made my confirmation. The sacrament of confirmation is like a spiritual coming of age for a young person in the Catholic Church. I was imbued with the power of the Holy Spirit and given the opportunity to choose an additional name. It made me feel significant and in charge.

I chose Daniel as my confirmation name. I felt it was a stronger name than Larry and a lot better than Lawrence, which I absolutely despised. (I also preferred it over my middle name Peter, which came to me from my paternal grandfather. I think it was probably my Uncle Joe's idea because, much to my irritation, he always called me Pete.)

Larry, at age 12, having just graduated from
8th grade and following his confirmation
at St. Roberts Catholic church.

Uncle Joe was my sponsor at my confirmation, and he stood proudly behind me during the ritual as the priest presided over my transformation into spiritual maturity and proclaimed my new name.

A couple of days afterward, I was outside playing in the yard when I heard a distant voice call someone named Daniel. Not me, I thought. Then the voice shouted for someone named Larry. It was not a voice I recognized, so I continued playing.

Coming closer, the voice sharply said "Pete, don't you hear me?" I realized then, to my chagrin, that it was my Uncle Joe.

My confirmation exercise opened up my mind and stirred in me new desires and questions. I was bothered by the attitude of certain people that God was somehow blessing me through my blindness and that I was an inspiration to them. I was held up to be one of God's perfect angels, and I resented this. I didn't want the image of me to be all angelic and good. I felt I was missing out. I didn't want people to see me as totally virtuous, a dedicated student and perfect little gentleman. This wasn't normal for a 12 year old, and I desperately wanted to be normal. I wanted to be mischievous, but I was afraid to be and I wasn't sure how.

I daringly played hooky from school a couple of times in 8th grade and sneaked off to Riverview, our local amusement park, with a friend. I started smoking, a habit that I continued until the age of 33. I wondered about my religion, the unbending doctrine of Catholicism and why some of my friends followed other religions. Who was right and why? This restless searching for spiritual answers haunted me throughout my teenage years and into young adulthood.

People invariably either feel sorry for blind people or feel inspired by them. Often, I have been approached by someone on the street who wants me to go to their church so that I can be healed.

They assure me that all that it will take is for me to believe it strong enough. "Brother Ralph can heal you. He has healed hundreds." Of course, that means that if I were to go and he doesn't heal me, it is my fault for not believing enough. Pretty convenient for Brother Ralph.

I used to be annoyed and amused by these offers, but now I try to explain that it is not my desire to be cured. This is shocking to people who are sighted. How could I not want to see, they ask? I guess the short answer is that since I have never had normal vision, I really don't know what I am missing. Perhaps a longer answer is that I have other health priorities more important to me. My hearing, which I have confidently relied on for independent travel, the gathering of information, communication and social interaction, has become impaired, and I am struggling with the inadequacies and limitations of electronic aids.

Several years ago I suffered a hip injury which has impaired my mobility. And so, gaining the ability to see is not at the top of my wish list. Also, I have heard that for someone who has never seen to suddenly be given sight, can be a very confusing and stressful experience.

WHO NEEDS A CANE?

I didn't believe in carrying a white cane when I was young. In fact, I didn't own one until I was a teenager in high school. It was easy for me to get around my neighborhood using my limited vision and memory. We had good sidewalks and little traffic.

To travel outside the neighborhood, however, I had to take hold of the arm of my brother, sister or a sighted playmate. This made me dependent on them, especially if we went to a distant or strange area. It was at these times that I discovered just how frustrating and vulnerable blindness could make me feel.

During the summer, we kids loved to go swimming at one of the local public swimming pools. The one closest to our house was at Portage Park, about 4 or 5 blocks away. I'd go there whenever my sisters, brother or one of my neighborhood playmates was willing to take me along. There were times when my sighted playmate and I would have a small disagreement over some trivial thing. He would then threaten to leave me by myself. This was very scary. Or he might decide to go off and do his own thing for a time, leaving me alone to stand there and wait.

I remember once waiting for over an hour for my friend Albert to come back for me at the swimming pool, not knowing that all the time he was just 20 feet away. I felt scared, angry and helpless. But, it was the price I had to pay for his taking me along in the first place. If I was tired or bored and wanted to leave the park, the beach or skating rink, I couldn't just get up and go. I had to wait until my sighted companion was ready to leave as well. If I wanted to go see a particular movie but my brother or playmate wanted to see a different one, we'd wind up going to the one they wanted.

I've continued to struggle with this dependency on sighted people all of my life. This need to ask or negotiate for favors from sighted colleagues, friends or family members has forced me to learn resignation, patience and flexibility. At times, even now, I resent the need to rely on my children or a friend to read things to me, to address an envelope for me or to drive me somewhere. I understand they are busy and have their own priorities. Still, I am jealous of their freedom.

One of the limitations imposed by blindness that most annoys me has to do with travel. Not being able to drive my own car means using taxis, the special Para transit service available in some cities for persons with disabilities or relying on friends or family. This means doing a lot of planning, persuading and negotiating. I am more patient now, more skilled as a negotiator and have come to realize that we all depend on each other, even though sighted folks may not see it that way. And yet, as well as I think I may have adapted to this problem, there are still those occasions when I feel frustrated, limited and vulnerable.

THE FOREST PRESERVE

Not far from our house on Montrose, at the northern end of the Milwaukee Avenue street-car line was the Edgebrook Forest Preserve. Going there when we were 12 and 13 was like traveling into the wilderness. A branch of the Des Plaines River meandered its way along, midst groves of silver elm, oak and birch. It was a slow-moving stream whose thick, pungent smell of decaying vegetation and sulfur discouraged any notion of satisfying one's thirst with a drink from its murky water.

We challenged each other to show off our bravery and agility by crossing to its opposite bank, hopping from slippery rock to tree root and back again without falling into the river. We imagined seeing wild animals, dangerous reptiles and hostile savages. We lived and played in that magic land of make-believe.

Years later, as young adults, we returned to the forest preserve to organize rowdy and carefree weekend weenie and marshmallow roasts with our friends. We sang and smoked, drank beer and celebrated our joy at being young. It was the best of times, even when it rained and our campfire went out and we had to pack up early and head home.

BY MYSELF

When my brother Jimmy or none of my play-mates were around, I played by myself.

I liked playing with clay because I could see the bright colors – red, green, yellow, blue. I molded them into soldiers: the red were the British, the green were the Germans, the yellow the Japanese, and the blue were us, the Americans. Using sticks from my Tinker Toy set as bayonets, the clay armies would engage in hand-to-hand combat. The blue and the red always won.

Like most kids, I loved playing with toy cars. My cars were made of sturdy metal or pewter, none of those flimsy plastic or aluminum cars that kids toy cars are made of today. These were strong and durable, great for crashing and smashing into each other.

For one of my birthdays, I got a steam-powered PT boat. The steam was generated by a lighted candle that heated water in a little pan in the cockpit of the boat. Two tubes ran from the cockpit to the stern. As the water began to boil, it sent steam down through the tubes and pro-pelled the boat along. It was pretty ingenious. I had a lot of fun playing with that boat in the bathtub.

At school, in woodworking class one semester, I built a neat-looking sailboat and a tie rack. We were taught by the instructor how to safely use shop tools.

Outside I played war games with imaginary enemies, practiced hitting rocks with my wooden bat and explored the prairie which extended all the way to the end of the block on both sides of our house. Out there, alone, midst the tall weeds and dandelions, I would sometimes become disoriented. Generally I could rely on the traffic sounds along Montrose Avenue to tell me where I was and what direction to take to head home. Montrose was my northern boundary. Facing Montrose, the alley was behind me. To my right, to the east was the corner gas station at Montrose and Central, and to my left, to the west beyond our house, was Major Avenue.

During winter, with snow on the ground, I could easily become disoriented. Snow muffles and absorbs sound. Snow is for a blind person what fog is for someone sighted. It happened one day that I was out playing, pretending to track a bear or wolf or something, and I got completely turned around. I had no notion which way was home. The wind was blowing hard, and I couldn't hear the traffic sounds on Montrose. I was cold, and it was getting dark. Which way to go? I decided to just pick a direction and start walking. At the worst, I knew I would wind up at the gas station at the far end of our block and have to turn around and walk all the way back. If I wound up walking south, I would reach the alley and know to turn to my right to head home. If it turned out that I picked north, I would come to Montrose Avenue and know that I had to turn left. And, if I was lucky enough to pick west, I would walk right into the side of our house. A good plan, I thought. So, I began walking.

The wind blew harder, and feathery snowflakes began licking at my face. I tried walking faster, but tripped and fell. I was 12 years old and close to crying. My face and hands were numb. I was scared and hungry and cold. What if I can't find the house? What if no one thinks to come looking for me? How long does it take for someone to freeze to death? Should I turn in a different direction? Should I yell for help?

Just then, I heard a voice. It was my mom. "Are you going to stay outside all night or are you going to come in for supper?"

"I'm coming in." I said with relief and joy. I had missed the side of the house by ten feet and was in our backyard. If I'd kept walking, I would have wound up at Major Avenue, a quarter block west of our house.

SHOPPING WITH MOM

S hopping with Mom was fun because she let me touch everything. Back then, during the 1940's, things were not sealed in plastic as they are today. You could actually feel what they were – toys, kitchenware, garden tools, costume jewelry, pencils, erasers, scissors, spools of thread, thimbles, combs and brushes, all sorts of things. My hands got to see what was there on the counters. Mom recognized that the best way for her blind child to learn about the world was by touch, and she never missed an opportunity to bring the world to my fingertips. A sailor's uniform, a policeman's badge, a circus clown's hat, a milk wagon horse, a fire engine – all were introduced to my inquisitive hands thanks to my mom's unembarrassed request and straightforward declaration: "He's blind. Touching things is how he sees."

Years later in college I tried using this same logic to convince the sorority ladies of Delta Gamma, who were my readers, about my special way of seeing, but they wouldn't buy it. Even when I explained to them that it was my mom's idea, they turned down my innocent request. I was hurt and disappointed.

Mom and I went food shopping at Hillman's in the basement of Sears. I loved the smells – freshly ground coffee, newly baked bread, fresh fruit and vegetables, the butcher counter which smelled of sausage and raw meat and fish.

My nose tells me a great deal about a place and about people. I love women who wear perfume, but not too much. I dislike the smells of stale cigarettes, unbathed bodies and unbrushed teeth. I love the pungent odor of printer's ink, the smell of a new car and the fragrance of freshly picked roses.

More than any other sense, smell arouses our emotions and stirs our memories. The tiniest whiff of an odor can evoke feelings of fear, sexual excitement or spiritual tranquility. A burning candle reminds me of being in church with my mom. The smell of clove takes me back to those unpleasant visits to the dentist when I was a kid. And, the fragrance of certain perfumes causes my heart to beat a bit faster as it reawakens in me treasured memories of a special someone.

Oddly enough, another smell which I enjoy, but one which causes the raising of eyebrows and provokes open laughter, is the smell of a skunk. Yes, a skunk. Not too close, but from afar. It reminds me of country, of the Wisconsin woods when I was a young teen at Boy Scout camp, happy and carefree, living close to nature.

Sounds also are especially important to a person who is blind. The sounds of traffic help us to navigate our way across a street. The sounds of voices help us identify the people who are present and where they are. The sound of a train whistle stirs memories of a journey taken or gives one the urge to pack a bag. Sounds I love – popping popcorn, the crunch of dry leaves under foot, the song of a cardinal, the waves from Lake Michigan crashing against the shore the orchestra of Guy Lombardo playing Auld Lang Syne. In later years, I have also learned to listen to and enjoy the sound of silence.

MAKING MUSIC

I was nine when Mom decided I should take piano lessons from the sisters at St. Roberts's parish. It was one of the two neighborhood Catholic churches near our home. The other was Our Lady of Victory. We divided our loyalties between them, going to church one Sunday at St. Roberts and the next to Our Lady of Victory.

My sisters and brother attended grammar school at St. Roberts, but Mom liked the other church too, because their Sunday service began 15 minutes later than the one at St. Roberts. It gave the family a little more time to walk the six blocks to the church. Yes, we walked to church. Mom didn't buy our first car until I was 12. Brother, those were really cold walks during the winter. Chicago is known as the windy city, and you definitely felt it during the winter months.

Going to church on Sunday was a must. Mom would bundle us all up in sweaters and coats, boots and mufflers, hats with earmuffs and warm gloves, and then march us along with cheery words. "This fresh air is good for you." There would be times when the wind blew so hard we could barely walk against it. When our noses and cheeks would begin hurting from the cold, Mom would say, "Turn around and walk backwards." It actually helped, and my brother Jimmy says that when he was young he could walk backwards just as fast as he could forwards.

Larry, Mom and Jimmy in the backyard on
Montrose, sitting on a large tree stump with a
prairie in the background. Mom is wearing a large
corsage which may mean it was Mother's Day.

Mom bought a second-hand piano so I could
practice on it. She also enjoyed playing the few
songs she remembered from when she was a teenager. It was my sister Eileen who, somewhat be-
grudgingly, took me to St. Robert's for my Saturday
morning piano lessons with the nuns.

About a year into my music career, the nuns
decided to put on a recital for the parents of their
young protégés. I was to perform a duet with a
girl named Maryellen. We were to play "She'll Be

Coming 'Round the Mountain When She Comes," sitting side by side at the same piano. I was petri- fied. I had never played in public, and I was ex- tremely shy around girls.

Until the day before the recital, we practiced separately. We had just one rehearsal together. Neither one of us said a word to the other. The re- cital went well. I remember Maryellen wore a deli- cious perfume that smelled heavenly. I felt that I was in love. I never told her how I felt though, and I never saw her again.

I recall another very embarrassing experience involving pretty girls when I was just seven. My mom took me to Alvernia high school, an all girls' school. The students there had transcribed a book of fairy tales into Braille, just for me. I don't remem- ber the name of it. What I do remember is being surrounded by a group of pretty girls – talking to me, hugging me, watching me. I was so embar- rassed. I could hardly wait to get out of there.

Shortly after the piano recital, the piano les- sons abruptly ended. I can't remember why, but Mom still had hopes of making me into a musician. She loved Dick Contino and Lawrence Welk. So, she decided that maybe I could learn to play the accordion like they did. My accordion teacher's name was Mr. Darrell. "It's like a barrel but with a D," he said. Neither he nor I knew braille mu- sic. I didn't even know there was such a thing as Braille music. So, half of the one hour lesson each

Bottom: Alvernia Braillists put slates and styluses aside when **Lawrence Johnson**, seven-year-old blind boy for whom they have brailled simple stories and fairy tales, comes to read to them. Standing behind Larry's desk is **Ruth Schneider**, who is brailling a prayerbook for Larry as a First Holy Communion gift. **Dorothy Rooney**, right, is a pleased and attentive listener.

Larry, at age 7, reading a story book transcribed for him into Braille by students from Alvernia High School.

week, Mr. Darrell spent dictating to me the notes and chords of the composition I was to learn. I wrote them down using my slate and stylus, creating my own braille music code. It was slow and tedious. Yet, Mr. Darrell had incredible patience.

The music school was located downtown and Mom and I had to take a bus and then the

Ravenswood "el." (In Chicago, that's short for elevated rapid transit train.) At North Avenue, we transferred to the subway. I loved riding the subway. The noise is deafening, but somehow also purifying. I wrote a poem about it once.

Approaching a subway entrance at street level, or standing and waiting on the subway platform, The cool wind from the trains pulling in and rushing out of the station was deliciously refreshing on a hot summer's day. While in winter, the temperature was always 15 to 20 degrees warmer down below than it was above ground.

I would be on the "El" going to my lesson when I would remember to take out the Emory board my mom had given me and file my nails down to the quick. "Always keep them short," Mr. Darrell would remind me. "You can't play well with long nails."

I studied with Mr. Darrell for about four years. I got pretty good. So good, in fact, Mr. Darrell decided that I was good enough to enter the city-wide competition of the annual Chicagoland Music Festival.

Reluctantly, I began putting in additional hours of practice. I didn't really want to follow a career in music. I preferred being outdoors playing baseball, kick-the-can or cowboys and Indians with my friends to staying inside practicing the accordion. But I did it for Mom. I surprised even myself by placing first in the preliminary round. With the finals just a month away, I dutifully practiced two hours every day.

Then, one afternoon, returning home with a gallon glass jug of milk from the neighborhood Mom and Pop store just a block away from the house, I stumbled, fell forward smashing the jug on the sidewalk and landed on the broken glass with my right arm. I ran home bleeding and crying. I had deep gashes above and below my right elbow about and inch and a half long and a quarter inch deep. Mom and my sister, Eileen, were on vacation in California. My sister Dorothy washed my wounds and put ice on my arm to stop the bleeding. Back in the 1940's, there was no 911, and people rarely thought about stitches or tetanus shots. Dorothy bandaged my arm as best she could. I couldn't bend the arm or practice on the accordion for the next two or three days because of the pain and for fear that the arm would begin bleeding again.

When I went to my music lesson the following week, Mr. Darrell showed his clear disappointment. He told me that one of the elements that the judges evaluated closely was form. This means that in playing the accordion, the right arm should be fully bent and held straight out to the side. With the wad of bandage wrapped around my elbow, it was quite impossible for me to do that.

The day of the festival came. I played the best I could. Needless to say, I did not do well. My mother and Mr. Darrell were deeply disappointed. He was kind and very consoling. He encouraged me to return for more lessons as soon as my arm was completely healed. But the moment had passed. My enthusiasm, what there was of it, had waned. Mom became resigned to the fact that her youngest son was not going to become a virtuoso after all. She agreed to discontinue my lessons and allowed me to play at my leisure, which I did from time to time sitting on a kitchen chair while she cooked dinner or, if the weather was nice, outside on our swing. She never tired of listening to me. Her favorite piece was a waltz called "Whispering Hope."

After nearly 60 years, I still have that accordion and occasionally take it out and try playing a few songs for my family or for my own nostalgic pleasure. One of the melodies that I still remember is the one that was my Mom's favorite. Coincidentally, it became my wife Diana's favorite as well. I played a recording of it at her funeral three years ago.

TWO TO TANDEM

B ecause we couldn't afford a car, Mom bought a bicycle and used to ride it to the store to buy groceries. Years later, my sister Eileen told me that it embarrassed her to see Mom riding the bike and that she would deny it was her mom when her girlfriends asked her about it.

When I was 10 or 11, Mom used to take me for long Sunday bike rides after church. I'd sit on the metal carrier behind her, with my feet dangling, not the most comfortable ride, but I enjoyed being with her and getting out. What made it more appealing was that we'd always stop for candy along the way. This may have been, in part, what motivated me some 40 years later to take up riding a tandem bike.

A tandem bike is a bicycle built for two. It has two seats, one behind the other and two sets of pedals. The rider in the front is known as the pilot and he/she does the steering, shifting of gears and breaking. The rider in the back is called the stoker, and he/she is supposed to concentrate on pedaling. Tandem bike-riding is now my favorite sport. The most I've ridden in one day is 100 km. (62.5 mi.). Very fatiguing. Usually my rides are much shorter, 15 miles.

My first biking partner was my friend Paul, who is quite a bit shorter than I. Biking along a park trail, Paul would sometimes forget to tell me about low-hanging branches. Consequently, I've learned to tell the difference between cedar bark and oak, by how they taste.

One of my most memorable biking adventures was a six-day, 135-mile trip, with six other tandem teams, down highway 35 along the Mississippi River. We slept in tents, cooked our own food and discovered just how large Minnesota mosquitoes can be. There is something indescribably exhilarating about coasting down a long hill against the wind at 35-40 mph. There is a sense of freedom, of peace and of harmony with nature.

Ten years ago, I had my first tandem biking accident. It happened just three blocks from our house. Cruising along at about 15 mph, a neighbor's dog suddenly darted out into the street right in front of our bike. We hit him and flew off the bike landing hard on the asphalt. I broke my right collarbone and shattered my right hip. I am now part bionic with a titanium hip joint which sets off the alarms at the airport security checkpoint. Oh yes, I am back bike-riding again. It's what Mom would have expected me to do.

MY DAD

I don't have many memories of my dad. Maybe that's why I didn't really miss him. After Mom separated from him and moved us to the house on Montrose, we kids would see him only occasionally on Sunday afternoons. He would call and we would go meet him at the drugstore on the corner of Montrose and Central. If he had money, he'd buy us an ice cream soda, but often he didn't. He'd give me a kiss, scratching my face with his stubble. He smelled of stale cigarettes, onions and beer. I remember him mostly talking to my sisters, Dorothy and Eileen, because they were older. These were not especially happy meetings for me. I went along with my brother and sisters not because I wanted to see him, but because I felt I was supposed to. I didn't actually resent him, like my brother Jimmy did, I just didn't see him as part of our family.

Mom never talked badly about our dad. In fact, she rarely talked about him at all. Whenever he did call, there would be that quick flash of resentment and annoyance in her voice, but she never refused him the chance to talk with us or meet us. There was one attempt at reconciliation. Dad came and spent one night, but they argued, and he was never invited back. I believe that by not having a father present in our home, a male role model, it took me a lot longer to mature. The Boy Scouts partially helped fill that void for me.

BOY SCOUTS

Mom got me into the Boy Scouts and sent me off to camp the summer I turned 12. It was exciting, but also scary. It was my first time away from home alone. During those two weeks at camp I learned about Indian lore, knot tying, sleeping on a canvass bunk in a tent and cooking over a camp fire. I had my first experience riding in a canoe. And I learned about those scary, achy feelings in the pit of my stomach caused by homesickness.

Boy Scout Troop 300 was made up entirely of visually impaired boys. Our scoutmaster, Howard Heldt, was a young lawyer, also visually impaired.

We were sponsored by one of the local Kiwanis clubs in Chicago and had our monthly meetings at a park district recreational center on the near north side. At these meetings we learned about scouting principles, how to send and receive Morse Code and about map-making. I earned one merit badge by making a detailed map of my neighborhood in braille using a tracing wheel, a large sheet of butcher block paper and my braille slate and stylus. On my map, I showed the drugstore at the corner of Montrose and Central, and right next to it, Kar's Dime Store, which was owned by an old Jewish couple who watched us kids like hawks to be sure we didn't try to steal anything. Going west from our house, a half block past Major Avenue was The Candy Store. Of course they sold a lot of other things besides candy, but we were most interested in licorice whips, Mary Janes, jawbreakers, black-jack gum – any and all of them for just a penny.

In scouts, we also learned about first aid and how to make a stretcher using our jackets and a couple of poles. One year we were invited to take part, along with several other scout troops, in a major scouting event at Soldiers Field, and we demonstrated our emergency scouting skills in front of an audience of several thousand spectators. It made us feel proud and important.

We were very lucky that our scout leaders were progressive-minded risk-takers. They looked for ways to challenge our abilities and introduce us to new experiences – experiences that as blind kids we would not normally have. As a scout, I had my first experience riding in an airplane. Two of us at a time were taken up in a Navy training plane for a short flight around the airfield. We had to put on parachutes and sit perfectly still behind the pilot. The noise of the plane was so loud I couldn't understand anything he said to us during the flight. I don't know what I would have done if he would have told us we had to jump. It was scary, but it was also very exciting.

Saturday mornings we were picked up by Red Cross volunteers and taken to the YMCA for swimming. Some of the kids were darn good swimmers and would swim laps. Because I didn't know how to swim, I stayed in the shallow part of the pool close to the edge. One of the Red Cross volunteers, a Mr. Stone, who drove us to the Y, would walk along the edge of the pool and playfully put his foot on my head and tell me to swim. This scared me even more. Nobody really tried to teach me to swim. The scoutmaster told me to hold on to the side of the pool and practice kicking. The water was cold and it wasn't much fun. What I did like was when we played a form of water polo. This consisted of our dividing ourselves into two opposing groups and trying to push a ball from one side of the pool to the other. There was a lot of grunting and shoving and dunking. At least, it made me feel that I was part of the group.

On one occasion, our scout master arranged to have a real diver's helmet brought to the Y to show us what it looked like. It had air hoses and a communication line. I remember it was extremely heavy, but in the water, with the air compressor going, it became quite buoyant. We were each given the chance to put it over our head and walk on the bottom of the pool to the far deep end. It felt quite scary. I remember thinking what if the compressor stops working or what if one of the hoses springs a leak? The scoutmaster gave us directions over the audio line, but the sound was so distorted, I couldn't understand a word he said. Going toward the deep end, the bottom of the pool was slippery and suddenly slanted at about a 45 degree angle. I almost lost my footing. It seemed to take forever to reach the far wall. When I did, I turned around and walked more quickly back. When I reached the slanted part, I got down on my hands and knees and crawled up it. At last, in the shallow part again, I stood shivering as the life guard lifted the huge helmet off my shoulders, and I told myself diving is definitely not for me. I am a Virgo, and Virgos like to keep their feet on land.

In the shower room, each shower had, in addition to the hot and cold water faucets, a separate high pressure cold water jet which you could activate by pulling a chain dangling overhead. Some of the older scouts, and occasionally the scoutmaster himself, would sneak up to us totally blind kids and pull the chain to give us a dousing of ice cold water. Being one of the youngest, I was often the brunt of their horse play.

From time to time, we were asked to perform our scouting skills and other talents for church groups and Kiwanis clubs. This ensured continued sponsorship and support. One of the skills that always seemed to amaze audiences was our ability to read braille numbers through various thicknesses of a handkerchief. People found it fascinating that we could distinguish the number and configuration of braille dots by touch. To be able to do so through 8, 16 and even 32 thicknesses of a handkerchief was truly astounding.

The following summer, just before the trip to Boy Scout camp, I got ringworm. The doctor prescribed a medication that turned out to be too strong and cause a second degree burn on my neck. So I missed the first week. It so happened that the scoutmaster broke his leg that summer and also missed the first week of camp. Fortunately for me, this meant that I could go with him to camp for the second week. That was the summer I was initiated into snipe hunting.

I was given a paper bag and a stick and taken to an open field where I was supposed to sit on the ground, cluck like a chicken and tap the stick on the ground. Eventually a small bird-like animal called a snipe would approach and crawl into the bag. At 13, you believe a lot of nonsense. So, I sat there and clucked and banged my stick on the ground. The scoutmaster and assistant scoutmaster took turns teasing me by answering my clucking call and approaching to within 20 feet before scurrying away. After about an hour, I realized the futility of my efforts and gave up. Back at camp, everyone had a good laugh at my expense.

Blind Scouts Enjoy Outdoors

(Story on page 1)

Blind Chicago Boy Scouts in baseball game at Owasippe camp near Muskegon, Mich. The batter, Larry Johnson, listens to the ba rolling toward him and prepares to hit it. Others are Robert Brink (left) and Wilburn Gilles.

Larry, at age 13, with Scout Troop 300 playing ground baseball with other visually impaired scouts.

One of our favorite activities at camp was ground baseball. Using a 12-inch baseball, we would roll the ball on the ground at the batter who, crouching down, would try to hit it by swinging his bat just above the ground. The pitcher would use fast balls and curves to try and strike out the batter. If the ball was hit, outfielders would try to block and catch the ball before it stopped rolling or passed the home run line. Players who had partial sight had a big advantage over those of us who were totally blind.

We also played football. One of the rules for this game was whoever carried the ball had to continuously call out, "I got it, I got it." Then everyone on the opposing team would converge on him to make the tackle. No passing was allowed. Brute strength was usually what prevailed. I remember once playing a frontline defensive position. The ball was handed off to their big fullback, Bob Louden, who came straight at me. At the time, I was 5 ft. 2 and weighed about 120 pounds. Bob was 5' 8" and weighed about 180. He knocked me down and ran right over me like a truck. After that, I decided no more playing front-line defense for me. It was safer to play back in the secondary and try hitting the ball carrier from the side.

On offense, I was pretty fast, and if I could manage to get past the front line defense, I could often outrun the secondary.

I remember one football game following a scout picnic in mid August. It was so hot, close to 100. We took frequent breaks to guzzle down cold bottles of soda pop. I think I set some sort of record that day, drinking 11 bottles of cream soda and root beer during that football game.

Our scout leaders were always thinking of new and fun things for us to do. One time we were teamed up with a Girl Scout troop for a scavenger hunt. Each of us was paired up with a sighted girl scout and sent out to find a list of things to bring back to the park field house by a given time. Some of my more daring buddies made the most of the adventure by managing to also find a little romance while searching in the park. My partner and I were too shy to try.

One winter our scout leaders arranged for us to have an ice skating party on the frozen-over lagoon in Humboldt Park. Now, I was great on roller-skates, but ice skating was something I just couldn't master. My sister Eileen said it was because I had weak ankles. I could barely stand up for ten seconds on ice skates before my feet would start to wobble and I'd fall over. So I stayed by the heater in the little hothouse built next to the lagoon while my fellow scouts went joyfully out on the ice. My friend Jack was a good skater and ventured far out on the lagoon ... too far. The ice in the middle of the lagoon was quite a bit thinner, and Jack fell through it and into the frigid water.

A park ranger and the assistant scout master pulled him out and brought him to the hothouse dripping and shivering. That ended the skating party.

SMOKING

I smoked my first cigarette when I was 12. I didn't like it, but I wanted to be accepted by my peers. I was too young to buy cigarettes, so I smoked OP's, that's other peoples, which meant I didn't smoke that often until I got into high school. In high school the older kids were able to buy cigarettes, so we bought smokes from them. At school, we did our smoking in the boys' bathroom. One time, Dennis and I were happily puffing away when our algebra teacher, Mr. Burke, walked in. He saw us and said: "Boys, that's bad for you." Then he did his business and left. He didn't report us. That was the way many grown-ups felt about teenagers and smoking. Neither they nor we knew how harmful it was. They just saw it as adolescent boys trying to act grown up, probably remembering that they did the same when they, themselves, were teenagers.

A pack of cigarettes, back in the 1940's, was a bargain, just 18 cents. We started out smoking Camels. But then we switched to Fatima, because they sponsored the radio show Dragnet, and it was one of our favorites. There were a lot of smokers who were role models for us – in the movies, in comic books and on the radio shows we listened to. Cowboys smoked. Soldiers smoked. Policemen and private detectives smoked. So, if these were our heroes, and we wanted to be like them, we too needed to smoke.

I tried, but never quite got the hang of blowing smoke rings. I could, though, light a cigarette out-side in a stiff wind on the first try. I switched brands of cigarettes many times. Let's see. There was Vermont Maple, which smelled like pipe tobacco. Parliament, that came in a fancy box and were filtered. Cools, that you smoked when you had a cold or sore throat, because they were flavored with menthol. English Ovals, they looked sophisti-cated. Girls and ladies especially liked them.

When I moved to Mexico, I began smoking much stronger, darker tobacco cigarettes – Delicados, Soberbios, with no filter. And that's when I began having problems with major cough-ing fits and with losing my voice. I switched to a pipe to see if that would help. it did somewhat. But I finally decided in the mid '60's, after 21 years of smoking, to completely quit. I'm glad I did.

IN THE KITCHEN

Patience, perseverance and determination were qualities Mom taught us every day, through her words as well as by her example. My accomplishments, whatever they have been, are a testament to her love, encouragement and support.

Mom had me help her in the kitchen. I think it was her way of making me feel useful and also to learn to do things I might need to know when I grew up. She put me to chopping spinach in a wooden bowl, snapping string beans, shelling walnuts or shucking our garden grown corn on the cob. My reward was to get to lick the bowl where she mixed the cake batter or the frosting.

These experiences encouraged my brother Jimmy and me to create culinary concoctions. We loved to make desserts with vanilla ice cream and chocolate pudding. And I'll never forget our first apple pie. We forgot to peel the apples. To keep Mom from finding out, we had to eat the whole pie between us before she got home. Needless to say, we didn't have much of an appetite for supper that night.

Mom taught me about gardening, cooking, making my own bed, cutting the grass, ironing, sewing and a hundred other household chores. She may have worried about my burning myself on the stove or with the iron, but she didn't show it. And so, thanks to her, today I am a fairly competent Mr. Fixit around the house and, if I do say so myself, a pretty darn good cook. My specialty is disguising and recycling leftovers into something my kids are willing to eat.

My culinary record is, however, not completely unblemished. There was the time, some years ago, when I decided to be a really thoughtful husband and prepare sack lunches for my wife, Diana, and me to take to work. Checking in the refrigerator I found this well-seasoned meat loaf and decided it would make wonderful sandwiches. So, I sliced and served it on bread, topped it with a little mustard and lettuce, wrapped the sandwiches and put them in lunch bags.

Diana was very pleased until she got to work and opened her lunch. It was then she discovered that I had made the sandwiches with raw meat loaf which she had seasoned and put in the refrigerator, planning to cook it for supper that night. She called to tell me, but it was too late. I had already wolfed down my cannibal burger. It actually tasted pretty good.

SCRAPES AND SCRATCHES

Mom encouraged me to get involved in everything – to be as normal a child as possible. She didn't believe in coddling me just because I happened to be blind. To the contrary, if I fell and scraped a knee or cut my finger and went crying into the house, she'd dry my tears, take me to the bathroom, run cold water over the injured area and then pour iodine over my wound. Can you remember what it feels like to have iodine poured over a freshly scraped knee? Well, after a couple of these first aid experiences, I decided that minor cuts and bruises really didn't need my mom's loving attention. It was, I believe, an important lesson in learning how to deal with pain and adversity, and I am grateful to her for that lesson. She was always there, of course, for the really serious things.

Mom pushed hard for my older brother and sisters to include me in their games and activities. I can still hear her saying: "Take Larry along with you," which they would reluctantly do. Yes, there was some resentment. But I don't believe it was any different than that expressed by my own children when I've forced them to play with their younger siblings. I received more than my share of bumps and bruises, cuts and scrapes. But my guardian angels (I'm sure I must have at least two) worked overtime and kept me from any serious injury.

FREE TO ROAM

During the school year our only real free time was on Saturday. But in the summer we were free to roam. We would leave right after breakfast and be outside with our friends the whole day, unless it was raining.

Our house on Montrose Avenue was the only one on the block and was flanked on both sides by wide open prairie. It provided lots of opportunities for us kids to play and to explore. Back then, no one worried about pedophiles or drug pushers or street gangs. Were we just naïve or were they, in fact, more wholesome, less dangerous times?

My friend David and his family lived on the floor above us. He was very tall (At age 12, he was already six feet) and a little clumsy. But he was my friend, because he would play with me. Outside, mostly we played war games. It was the early 40's, during World War II. We were the good guys fighting against the Germans or Japanese. We improvised a lot. Rocks became hand grenades and sticks became rifles, bazookas or bayonets. There were a couple of trees in the backyard that came in handy as look-out posts to spot enemy planes. We captured prisoners, blew up tanks and shot down attacking airplanes.

Other times, we tied a rubber tire to one of the tree's thick branches and played Tarzan and the Apes. We fought leopards and lions and cheetahs. We also used it as a horse when we switched to playing cowboys and Indians. We didn't have a lot of toys, no television, computer games or DVD's, so we had to use our imaginations. Kids today don't know how to use their imagination and because of it miss out, I think, on having some of the best fun.

David's uncle was named Lawrence. He was a kind of handyman but a bit odd. He lived in the attic above David and his family. My brother Jimmy told me that the attic had no electricity and that Lawrence used a kerosene lamp for light. Jimmy worried that he might one day set the attic on fire. Lawrence did have one talent. He played the harmonica. But the only melody we ever remember him playing was "Home on the Range."

Our other playmates lived mostly on Pensacola, the next street south of us. Johnny, Albert and the twins lived along Pensacola. Marty lived two blocks over.

Donnie and Joey Oaker lived down the alley from us. Their dad was a very kind and generous man who knew we were poor and gave us toys. One day we learned that he had been killed, run over by a garbage truck. We felt very sad. We didn't see much of Donnie or Joey after that. I think they moved away.

The alley, our alley, ran behind our house and all along the backyards of the houses that faced Pensacola. The alley was our trail to travel between each other's houses. We never knocked on doors or went around to the front. We'd stand in our friend's backyard and yell at the top of our lungs "Yo Albert! Yo Al!" Either our friend or his mom would soon open the door and let us know if he was able to come out and play.

We played cops and robbers, war games and a lot of baseball and football. There was no beeping baseball as there is now. I went by the sound of the baseball hitting the ground or the other players running with the football. I admit I occasionally did tackle players on my own team, especially my brother. And that wasn't always by mistake. Since he is a year and a half older than I, he always got the better of me in our frequent sibling fights. So, tackling him on the football field was sort of my way of accidentally getting even.

But Jimmy and I did play a lot together. I would hit a baseball to him so he could practice catching ground balls, fly balls, pop-ups. Rarely was I ever able to hit it over his head. We also played football, designing clever pass plays. He would shift the football to me and then run down the field, cut to his right or left or come back to me according to our prearranged plan. We used this quite effectively when we played two-man football against Marty and Albert. Sometimes I'd fake the pass and then run straight ahead with the ball, and Jimmy would block for me. Jimmy and I almost always won. He was sure-handed and fast, and our deceptions worked the majority of the time.

One winter Jimmy and I built an igloo next to the dilapidated garage in our back yard. The snow was piled high next to the garage, so we just packed it down and added more. Then we began hollowing it out and eventually made it big enough for both of us to crawl inside. It was amazingly warm in there out of the wind.

Of course, we also had sleds. There weren't any hills close to our house, so we would run as hard as we could holding the sled in front of us and then belly flop with it and let momentum carry us through the snow. Other times we would go to the park where there were a couple of hills, climb to the top with our sleds and then coast back down. A couple of times I went with Jimmy to a place where the Park District people built a toboggan slide. It was high, maybe 50 feet tall and slick. Wow! Going down that slide was really scary, but fun.

One Christmas, both Jimmy and I were given chemistry sets. I guess all kids enjoy doing experiments, discovering how things work. We learned that by mixing certain chemicals together in a beaker and heating the mixture over a Bunsen burner we could produce interesting reactions. We made various dyes, invisible ink, percussion crystals that would explode when thrown on cement pavement, and phosphorescent solutions to apply to our toy cars and airplanes so that they would glow in the dark. We learned that different chemicals produced different colors when burned – barium and copper sulfate for green, strontium or iron sulfate for red, sodium for yellow and magnesium for brilliant white. I still had enough vision then that I could appreciate and enjoy the colorful consequences of our experiments.

Fireworks were technically illegal in Chicago. We had to go outside the city limits to purchase them, which in our case, was less than a mile. So, every Fourth of July, we bought an assortment of sky rockets, cherry bombs (the big daddy of fire-crackers back then) lady fingers (for sissies and girls), Roman candles and a variety of fountains, flares and sparklers. I enjoyed shooting off fire-works, lighting sparklers, colorful fountains and watching those magical snails that seemed to crawl along the sidewalk.

Along with Jimmy, I lit my share of cherry bombs and placed them under tin cans. Though I couldn't see how high they flew, I'd count to see how many seconds it took for them to land. Was it risky? I guess so. In fact, I knew one kid in our high school that became blind because of fireworks. But I was already blind, so that was no deterrent.

At the end of the alley, alongside the house on the corner was a row of raspberry bushes. Lying on our backs under the bushes, out of sight of the home owner, those juicy red berries were a deli-cious midday snack. I only remember her catching us once. Neighbors really didn't mind our friendly trespassing to snag an apple off a tree, munch a few raspberries or quench our thirst with a drink of water from a garden hose. Lunchtime we would show up at any one of our friends' houses and be assured of getting a sandwich, a few cookies and a glass of milk.

On rainy days we'd play down in someone's basement. One of the guys had an electronic baseball game with marbles. That was a lot of fun. We also played monopoly, Chinese check-ers and card games like war, fish and black jack. Marty used to wonder why I always beat him in black jack until he figured out that I could read the braille number on the corner of the cards as I dealt them to him. He got even with me though in a game we used to play bouncing a ball off his front steps. He would hit the ball on the edge of the step to make it fly over my head for a home run. Marty's mom did not work, so lots of times during the summer we'd go to his house for lunch or cookies and milk. Most of our friends' moms didn't work. Back then, families could get by on just one income, and neighbors watched out for each other and kept an eye on us kids. Doors were never locked. We could leave a bicycle on our front lawn overnight and it'd be there in the morning. A neighbor might borrow a cup of sugar and then bring it back a couple days later with a plate of cookies.

Catching fireflies and putting them in a jar was a great way to spend a summer evening.

Sometimes we'd get together in somebody's basement and create fantasy adventures. At times we'd just talk out the parts, and other times we'd act them out. We could be any characters we wanted to be – Superman, Batman, Captain Marvel, Flash Gordon or the "Torch." Mostly the characters were comic book heroes. My brother

Jimmy was a great collector of comic books. Often, he would read them out loud to me. We'd create some really exciting crisis situations for our heroes and then figure out a way to get them free again. We played both the good guys and the bad guys, and we'd add in the sound effects to make it more realistic. It was great fun and great for developing our imaginations, which has come in quite handy for me in making up bed-time stories for my six children and 20 grandchildren.

A DOG FAMILY

Jim, age 9, & Larry, age 8, with dog Pepper
in backyard of house on Montrose.

W e were definitely a "dog" family. I remember a steady succession of 4-legged friends, a brown shepherd we named Rex, a couple of terriers we called Pepper. My older sister, Dorothy, was the one who was always "finding" dogs who needed a home.

Because we allowed them to run free, a couple of them got hit and killed by cars. There would be a period of mourning, and then Dorothy would show up with a new K9 orphan who quickly became our pal. Our dogs would try and follow us when we went off to play baseball, and we'd try and shoo them back home. During the summer they entertained themselves by chasing after the wild rabbits that lived in the adjacent prairie. Only once do I remember that one of our Peppers caught a baby rabbit. I think he was as surprised as we were, and we scolded him harshly.

RADIO SHOWS

M y favorite hobby as a kid was listening to the radio. Back in the 1940's, there was a whole line-up of after-school adventure shows from 4:30 to 6:00 p.m. every day on the radio for kids. There was Captain Midnight, Buck Rogers, Terry and the Pirates, Little Orphan Annie, Sky King, Jack Armstrong and, after the 6 PM news the

Lone Ranger. I drank Ovaltine and ate Wheaties, Cheerios and Quaker Puffed Wheat "shot from a gun" to support my radio program heroes and to get the box tops I needed to enter those innumerable contests and to send in for my secret decoder rings and glow-in-the-dark insignias. I'm sure that this is where I developed my strong desire to become a radio announcer.

Radio was a major source of entertainment for the whole family. During the daytime, there were a slew of serialized dramas for stay-at-home moms. The programs were sponsored mostly by soap manufacturers and became known as "Soap Operas." In the evenings, there were comedy shows like Burns and Allen, Jack Benny, Amos and Andy, Red Skelton, Fred Allen, Baby Snooks and Edgar Bergen and Charlie McCarthy. There were scary half-hour shows like Lights Out, Inner Sanctum and Suspense. There were quiz shows like Truth or Consequences, People Are Funny, You Bet Your Life with Groucho Marx and The 64 Dollar Question (back when a dollar was really worth something). There were Hollywood movies adapted for the radio, which featured leading Hollywood movie stars, like the Mercury Radio Theater and the Monday night Lux Radio Theater. It was truly the Golden Age of radio, and today some radio stations are delighting audiences by bringing back Old-Time radio shows.

SATURDAYS WERE SPECIAL

Saturday mornings featured the radio show Let's Pretend, a dramatized 30 minute presentation of all our favorite fairy tales. Saturday night was the Lucky Strike Hit Parade and bath night. We all took turns. Mom would add boiled water heated on the stove to keep the bath warm as we took turns. Being the youngest, I was last. In the winter, Mom would connect an electric heater in the bathroom so we wouldn't shiver to death as we were toweling off.

If we could scare up the 12 cents admission, my brother, Jimmy, David or some other friend and I would go to the Saturday matinee movies at the Patio, the Gateway or the Jeff to take in a western or horror film. Jimmy was pretty good about describing the action so that I could fully enjoy the film. I think that movies back then had more dialogue and logical scene changes that made it easier for a blind child to follow what was happening. Then too, western plots were pretty predictable. I often knew what was going to happen before it happened. On the way home or back at the house we'd play act scenes from the movie. We'd scare ourselves with stories of vampires and mummies and Frankenstein monsters and werewolves. Again, we played all the parts and imagined the others. Being the oldest, Jimmy would always want to play the part of the hero. David or I got to be the monster or the monster's victim.

Today, people don't like it if you talk during a movie. So, I rarely go to the movies any more. Instead, I'll wait until the movie I'm interested in comes out on video, and then I'll rent or buy it and watch it at home. This has an advantage. If the action is too fast or if I can't follow a scene, my sighted companion can stop the tape, explain it, rewind the tape and play it again.

Some movies on video now come with a recorded audio description. These are wonderful for visually impaired persons. A narrator or commentator gives short descriptive remarks about the visual action, the scenery and the actor's movements or gestures during natural pauses in the dialogue. It precludes the need for a sighted person to sit with me when I want to watch a movie on video. Some programming on television is now also audio-described. It can be heard over the secondary audio channel (SAP) available on newer television sets.

HALLOWEEN

As a kid one of my favorite times of the year was Halloween. I'd go out with Jimmy, David or one of my other playmates, or we would go out as a group "trick-or-treating" throughout the neighborhood. We would make it a three-day affair–starting the day before Halloween and ending our canvassing for treats the day after.

We had our stories all rehearsed. If it was the day before Halloween, we'd tell the people that our parents were taking us out of town to visit our uncle and aunt the next day and so we wouldn't be able to come by. Then, the day after Halloween, we'd go to a different area of the neighborhood and tell the people that our moms kept us home the previous day because we had a fever. It always worked, and often we'd receive coins instead of candy, which was our intent. We'd stop people coming out of the store or walking along the sidewalk and say "Trick or Treat." Most of the time they were good-natured about it. They'd smile and hand over a few pennies. Those pennies added up. We'd average maybe two or three dollars over that three-day period, serious money for kids back in the 1940's. I'll bet we walked ten miles making our rounds. Of course, we also did pea-shooting at windows and street lamps, soaped store windows and dumped over garbage cans. I remember once David and I got caught dumping over a garbage can, and we had to load all that smelly garbage back into the can. Orange peels, egg shells. Yuck, that was no fun.

RIVERVIEW

Riverview. There was nothing like it ... the most wonderful of all amusement parks. At the intersection of Belmont and Western Avenue, a place for innocent fun and entertainment.

We kids could hardly wait for it to open each year around Memorial Day. I was probably 10 or 11 when Mom took us there for the first time.

There were all kinds of rides, some scary like Spook Town, Aladdin's Castle, Hades and the Jitterbug House. There were exciting roller-coaster rides like the Silver Flash, the Blue Streak, the Comet and the king of all roller-coasters the Bobs. I didn't venture on to these tummy-turning rides until I was older and braver, around 13.

There were also tamer rides for those less brave like the Caterpillar, the Tilt-a-Whirl and the Mill-On-The-Floss. The Caterpillar was a series of cars, linked together that followed a circular route around a platform, and as they did so, a cloth cover would come down and cover them. The Mill On The Floss was a more generic name for the Tunnel of Love. People, couples mostly, sat in a flat bottom boat and a slow current propelled them along a covered passage that made them feel as if they were passing through a deep cave. We liked it because it was cool there in the tunnel away from the hot summer sun. Later, when I was old enough to know better, I took a pretty young lady for a romantic ride and stole a kiss in the dark.

Jimmy and I kept count of how many different rides we were brave enough to try. I loved the Dodgem's, where you got to drive your own bumper car, and the Flying Scooter, where you moved a tiller from side to side; it gave you the feeling of flying an airplane. As we got older, we were allowed to go to Riverview alone or with friends.

Mondays, Wednesdays and Fridays were two-cent days. That meant you could go on any ride in the park, except the Bobs and the Parachute, for just two cents. We would save up all the pennies we possibly could, do errands for neighbors, collect all the returnable bottles we could find and take them to the store for refunds, and beg our mom for a few extra cents so we could go to Riverview for the whole day. Sometimes we'd walk the 4-1/2 miles from our house to Riverview in order to have more money to spend on the rides, for snow cones and for other snacks or to spend at the penny arcade to get baseball cards for our collections. (I sure wish I had kept some of those baseball cards. Some are worth big money today.)

Our mom worked as a cashier at the turnstiles a couple of years, and so did my sister Dorothy. And my brother Jimmy worked the summer he was 16, operating the kiddie rides. He says that he hated polishing all those brass rails on the merry-go-round that little kids were forever getting "stickied up" with their cotton-candied hands.

Riverview, of course, had its share of shooting galleries, fortune tellers and freak shows. But those didn't interest us much. Each year we would look for new rides had been added and old rides that were taken down. One of the new additions that I remember I enjoyed, but whose name I've since forgotten, was shaped like a barrel. A certain number of people were allowed on the ride. We stood with our backs to the wall. The barrel began spinning faster and faster. The centrifugal force pushed and held us against the wall. Then, the floor dropped away. We felt like flies glued to the wall. At the end, when the ride began to slow, the floor came back up and everyone fell into the center of the barrel screaming and laughing.

Another favorite of ours was Shoot-the-Chutes, a boat ride. It was as popular with spectators as it was with riders. Boats carrying twenty or so people were hoisted up to a platform, six stories high or so, and then let lose to plunge down a watery slide. The ride ended when the boat splashed into a small lagoon at the bottom of the slide, soaking the occupants and some of the spectators, who screamed in delight.

Childhood memories always seem magnified as we look at them in retrospect. Nevertheless, for me, Riverview will always be the World's Greatest Amusement Park. We spent so many happy afternoons, from noon to 5 PM, walking around its 2-1/2 mile midway, spending our pennies cautiously, caught up in the carnival atmosphere, the smells of popcorn and hot dogs, the roar of the roller-coasters overhead, the blaring music and the throngs of people, just like us, out for a few hours of wholesome fun.

Riverview closed at the end of the 1967 season after 64 years. It marked the end of an era. But it will never be forgotten by those of us who had the joy of being there and experiencing it.

CHRISTMAS TIME

I loved Christmas. What kid doesn't? A few days before, we'd go shopping for our Christmas tree, a live Christmas tree. Holiday merchants would bring in a truckload of Scotch pines or Douglas firs and set up shop in an open field next to a gas station, and all of us kids would go with Mom to look at the trees. We'd pick out a six or seven-footer, inspect it from all angles, pulling down the branches to see just how full and fresh it was. It needed to last until New Year's. Then Mom would haggle with the salesman over the price. Fifty to 75 cents was our limit. In those early years, we didn't have a car, so it meant we had to drag our tree three or four blocks through the snow to our home. That was part of the fun, even when it was 10 degrees Fahrenheit, and a strong wind was blowing from the north.

When we got the tree home, we struggled to stand it up tall and straight in the sturdy, iron tree stand. With Eileen and me holding the tree, Mom and Dorothy would stand back and direct which way to lean it. Then Jimmy would turn the three screws of the stand until they bit into the bark and held the tree firmly in place. Next we carried it into the house and stood it in the living-room by the front window. The clean, fresh fragrance of pine floated in the air.

Decorating the tree was everybody's job. Even I got to hang tinsel, candy canes and some colored glass balls on the lower branches. Eileen and Dorothy checked and rechecked the sets of colored lights, making sure to remove any burnt out bulbs before stringing them artistically among the branches. A magnificent blue star was fastened to the very top, while a tiny village emerged on a cotton snow landscape underneath, with houses, animals, a church and a little electric train running its Figure 8 course.

There was also a special place for the manger— the Holy Family, the shepherds, the donkey, the wise men and their camels. All was done with pride and love and joy.

Sometime after midnight on December 24th, Santa managed to squeeze himself down our ten-inch stove pipe and deposit presents under the tree for all of us. We were up at first light of day excitedly ripping away the wrapping paper from the toys and games and clothes which St. Nick had marked with our names.

Our play would be interrupted as Mom marched us off to church and then back home for Sunday dinner–roast chicken, pork or "roll-ups" (also known as pigs in the blanket). These are thin slices of beef, about two inches square, wrapped around a slice of bacon and held firmly in place with a toothpick and roasted in the oven or cooked with potatoes and other vegetables in a pressure cooker. Yummy!

The girls would do the dishes, while Jimmy and I went off to show our friends what Santa had brought us and to see what they had received.

After New Year's we took down the tree, carefully removing and boxing all the ornaments, icicles, tinsel and lights. Then we dragged it out the front door and around to the backyard where we set it ablaze. What a wonderful smell that is–burning pine. I've heard that they use pine in crematoriums. In a strange morbid way, maybe that's another reason why, when I die, I've decided I want to be cremated.

FUN ON WHEELS

My 10th Christmas was when Santa brought me a brand-new beautiful red tricycle. I had a really small one for a kid five or six years old, which I found abandoned in the prairie on our block. I had to squat down to be able to ride it. But my new bike, okay "trike" was high off the ground. I felt proud and tall sitting on it. My feet barely reached the sidewalk. I raced the neighbor's kids on their bicycles and could almost keep up with them. I never questioned why Santa had brought me a three-wheeler instead of a two-wheeler. Maybe it was because I felt safer and more confident on three wheels.

Jimmy had a scooter that I borrowed from time-to-time. I liked it a lot because of its maneuverability. In our neighborhood, there were sidewalks along every block, separated from the street by three feet of grass or lawn. I had just enough vision to be able to distinguish the green of the grass, the gray sidewalks and the black tar top of the street. So, I used my limited vision, my hearing and my sense of direction to travel around our block.

Roller-skating was another popular outside activity. The kind of skates we had were those that clamped on our shoes. They had a strap that came around the ankles and a clamp on the front that tightened, with the help of a skate key, against the toe of the shoe. We always carried the key in our pocket, because the skates would often get loose as we skated over grass or gravel or uneven sidewalks. Then we'd have to stop and tighten them again or risk having them come off, causing us to fall on our face. The length of the skates could be adjusted to fit different sizes of feet. So, one pair of skates might be shared by two or more kids in the same family. We also used roller-skates to make homemade scooters. Oranges came in wooden crates, and we found those crates to be ideal for constructing our own version of a scooter. We'd use one board and attach two roller-skates, one behind the other to a 2x4 board. Then we'd nail a crate atop the board and add wood handles. The crate protected us in crashes and was used to carry stuff. Much later I learned about roller-skates that we could put on like shoes and I also learned about indoor roller rinks.

WILBUR

One interesting aspect of my elementary school experience was the special travel guide or attendant program. Under this program one of the eighth grade students was assigned to a blind student to take him/her back and forth to school on regular public transportation. There were only three elementary schools in the city of Chicago where blind students could attend. This meant that we had to travel rather long distances to school and change buses two or three times each way. It was excellent mobility training.

The unusual aspect of this travel/attendant program was that the students selected to be our guides were from the special class of hard-of-hearing students. I suppose this was because they also lived a long distance from the school. The incentive for these students was that their bus fare was paid for by the school.

Wilbur, who was hard of hearing, was my attendant/guide in the 8th grade. We were a rather daring duo. I loved to run with him to catch the Montrose Avenue streetcar just as it would be pulling away. It was one of those old style streetcars in which the back end was open. At Wilbur's signal, I would reach out, grab the handrail and swing aboard. It was a little dangerous, but it made me feel like one of my cowboy heroes.

When I first started riding the bus it was three cents for half fare and seven cents for full fare. Montrose Avenue had a street car which ran from Broadway to Milwaukee Avenue. There we changed to a trolley bus which continued to Naraganset. Later they removed the street car tracks and the trolley bus replaced it. It was, I suppose, because it was more maneuverable than the old streetcar.

Wilbur owned a motorbike. Sometimes after school we would take rides together, with me sitting on the carrier in the back. Once, after a lot of persuading, Wilbur agreed to let me try and steer with him sitting behind me giving directions. Well, we got about 30 feet down the block and then crashed into a parked car and went sprawling on to a neighbor's lawn. After that, Wilbur insisted on doing all the steering.

I was a very good student and a quick learner in elementary school. My teachers decided to skip me two half grades, half year in 5th grade and half year in 7th. It was quite an honor, but I'm not sure it was a good idea. I think it made it a lot harder for me socially and psychologically. As a result, my classmates were all a year to a year and a half older. By nature I was very shy around girls and to be a year younger made me feel even more awkward and unsure of myself. I never had a girlfriend in elementary school. But I had a big crush on a girl in my eighth grade class. Her name was Angela. She was 13, and I was 12. She was smart, kind of shy, blonde and, according to Wilbur, very pretty. If I said three words to her in class, that was a lot.

One day I plotted with Wilbur to find out where Angela lived by following her home. Leaving school, we boarded the same Kedzie Avenue streetcar as usual and got off at Montrose. Normally Wilbur and I would cross Montrose and wait for the westbound streetcar while Angela and her girl friend took the eastbound one. This time, we crossed Kedzie and waited with Angela and her girlfriend to take the eastbound streetcar. The girls were surprised and asked where we were going. I lied and said I was going to visit my grandmother. The streetcar came, and we got on.

Wilbur and I sat a few seats away from the girls. Wilbur wore one of those old style hearing aids which had a large microphone/amplifier that he carried in his shirt pocket. Because Wilbur was hard of hearing, he didn't know how loud he was speaking. I was anxious to find out what my dream girl was wearing, so I leaned over and speaking softly into Wilbur's microphone, I asked him. "Tell me what Angela is wearing."

Wilbur responded in a voice loud enough for everyone on the streetcar to hear: "Oh, Angela looks really pretty, Larry in her pink dress with white flowers, and she has a cute little pink bow in her hair."

I knew both girls were now looking at me, and my face turned crimson. I wanted to crawl under the seat. I heard the girls giggle. I nudged Wilbur and said, "Come on, let's get off."

As we passed by Angela and her girlfriend, they both said, "Bye Larry. Say hello to your grandma for us." And then they giggled again. I was too embarrassed to reply.

ROCK-OLA STADIUM

Rock-ola Stadium was a softball park two blocks from our house and home to a professional girls' softball team called the Rock-ola Music Maids. The girls played with a 12-inch hard ball and used gloves. They had ten players on a team, the usual nine plus a short center fielder who usually played behind second base. Bubbles

Donahue was the short center fielder for the Music Maids, and she was one of their stars. Many of the girls were gorgeous and very athletic.

In our early teens, Jimmy and I started sneaking in to watch the Friday night games. We would walk along the outfield fence until we found a spot where there was a small gap between the bottom of the fence and the ground. Then we bent the fence upward while digging out the dirt below. Eventually, we made a space large enough for us to wriggle underneath the fence and on to the field. Keeping in the shadows we worked our way around to the stands and sat to enjoy the game.

Park security discovered our hole in the fence and tried to thwart our illegal entry by spreading baseline chalk all over the ground by our entrance. We realized that if we showed up in the bleachers with chalk dust on our clothes, we would be discovered. So, we returned home, collected some old newspapers and returned to lay them on top of the chalky ground. Now we could again slide safely under the fence.

A few weeks later, park maintenance people repaired the fence by staking it to the ground. Oh well, only one option left. Instead of going under, we would have to climb over. Persistence pays off.

When he was 13, Jimmy began working at Rock-ola first as batboy and then later selling popcorn and peanuts. So, he got to get in legally.

That meant I had to persuade Albert or David to go with me to the games.

Besides the girl softball games, Rock-ola Stadium also hosted an annual 4th of July fireworks display and a donkey baseball event. Yes, I mean baseball played on donkeys. It was pretty hilarious. Only the pitcher and catcher didn't have to use donkeys. The batter, after hitting the ball, had to get on his donkey and ride him to first base. Except the donkey didn't usually want to go there. Meanwhile the fielders had to chase the ball riding their donkeys. One batter, out of frustration with his donkey's stubbornness, got off the donkey, picked up the animal and jogged around the bases carrying his donkey to home plate. It probably wasn't legal to do it that way, but the crowd loved it.

THE KLEVENS

When David and his family moved away, the Klevens moved in. They had three girls Shirley, Marilyn and Iverna. Shirley and Marilyn were older - around Dorothy and Eileen's age. Iverna was older than me but younger then Jimmy. It was a real disappointment to have my pal David replaced by a girl. Iverna wasn't much good at baseball and didn't like playing war games or cowboys and Indians. Mr. Kleven would often come home drunk. And then he'd yell at his wife and kids and slap them around. We could hear the commotion upstairs. Sometimes the mother and the girls would come down to our flat and hide when Mr. Kleven was on one of his rampages.

Mom and Mrs. Kleven became very good friends. And, when we moved to Lawndale at one point Mrs. Klevin and Iverna stayed with us. They slept upstairs in the bedroom next to mine. I didn't mind, I thought of Iverna more like a sister.

JOHN MARSHALL HIGH SCHOOL

I began high school at the age of 13, a year younger than most of my classmates.

I was short, skinny and shy. I had strong values of morality learned from my Catholic upbringing and reinforced through the radio shows I used to listen to–the Lone Ranger, Tom Mix, Jack Armstrong, Terry and the Pirates. Honesty, loyalty and bravery were the principle character traits of these radio heroes of mine. They showed kindness and compassion toward the weak, strength and resolve toward the unjust and gentleness and chivalry toward the fairer sex. Yes, I lived in a world of romantic idealism and innocence.

There was just one high school for visually impaired students in Chicago, John Marshall High, on Adams and Kedzie. At first, we were transported to and from school by collective taxi. Later it was by bus, share-riding with other "handicapped" students from Spalding School, also known as the "crippled" school.

Mr. Morganstein was the driver of the taxi that picked up five of us blind students each day during the first three years that I attended John Marshall. He was a staunch Chicago Cubs fan, and the Cubs, like my White Sox, were almost always in last place. Once Mr. Morganstein took me to a Cubs game and, as predicted, they lost. Throughout that season, we had a friendly ten cent bet on all the Cubs' games. I came out quite a bit ahead. I think he knew I would.

In high school, all our classes were integrated "mainstreamed," while our "home room" had three special resource teachers to assist some 25 visually impaired students. Many of the books we had to use were not available in Braille or recorded format. There were regular workbook assignments in algebra, English, science and social studies. Three special teachers were simply not able to provide all the sighted reading assistance that was required. So, a unique sighted student reader assistance program was set up. Sighted classmates were encouraged to volunteer as readers just as they might do as hall monitors, attendance aides, etc. They received service points according to the number of hours they volunteered and, upon graduation, were presented with special certificates of recognition.

It was a wonderful program–an opportunity for us blind students to meet and get to know our sighted peers one-on-one. It frequently resulted in the making of some new friendships, as well as the blossoming of some teenage romances. It was a very important element in my socialization and personal development.

We played a lot of baseball in high school but it was a different kind of baseball. Our field was long and narrow, about 30 ft. wide and perhaps 75 ft. long. There was a fence along the left side and the school building on the right. Batters would hit the ball, a 14-inch softball, themselves by throwing it up into the air and batting it. Once the ball hit the ground, the fielders would try to pick it up before it stopped bouncing or rolling. If they did, that would constitute an out. However, if the ball stopped rolling before a fielder could pick it up, then it would be a hit. Depending on where the ball stopped, it would be scored a single, double or triple. A homerun would be scored if the ball hit or went past the back fence. We chose teams and were quite competitive. If a player hit the ball over the fence on the left, it was an automatic three outs for that team. One trick some of us tried was to hit the ball against the left fence and cause it to die immediately, scoring a single. Since I was not a power hitter, that was my strategy. We played every chance we could, during our lunch hour and in place of Physical Education class.

Because of the neighborhood where it was located, 90% of the students who attended John Marshall High were Jewish. This meant that on Jewish holidays, like Rosh Hashanah, Yom Kippur and Hanukkah, there would be only about 10% of students in attendance. Frequently we would be excused from class and permitted to go out and play baseball the whole day. What joy!

Winter months, we played a special brand of basketball in the gym. In reality, it was more like a combination of football, soccer and wrestling. The only time when the coach would call a "time-out", was when he would announce "There's blood on the ball." It was a grueling 40-min. workout, but loads of fun.

One semester we joined the ROTC. I'm not sure why. I don't think anyone seriously considered us becoming officer candidates for the military. More likely it was a substitute for taking PE. Most of our ROTC training consisted of doing a variety of boring calisthenics. One time though, we actually got to shoot a rifle at a rifle range in the school basement. The .22 caliber rifle was a real gun. Boy, it made a lot of noise down in that cavernous basement target range. Afterwards, they let us collect some of the spent shells to take home. Can you imagine any school district today allowing blind kids to handle and shoot a firearm?

Just like all other kids in school, we wrote notes to each other in class. Our notes were, of course, in braille but also in code, just in case the class-room teacher should decide to confiscate them and show them to one of our home room teach-ers who knew braille. We were pretty ingenious about it. In one of our secret codes, we wrote the letters backwards. In another, we assigned each letter a number and wrote the message all in numerals.

In Boy Scouts several of us learned the Morse Code and were pretty good at it. So much so, that we used it in class to send messages and help each other with the right answer when called upon by the teacher. Dennis, Bill, Bob, Albert and I were the principle members of this communica-tions network. Dennis sat in front of me and Bill behind me. Bob and Albert were in the row next to us. When the teacher asked a question of one of us, and he couldn't quite remember the cor-rect answer, there would be a flurry of silent taps on the shoe from the guy in front or across from him or pokes on the back from the guy behind. It worked amazingly well. Somehow the teacher never caught on, or if she did, allowed it to hap-pen anyway.

George was very studious and very serious. So, he became the brunt of one of our classroom practical jokes. In English class, George sat in the first desk, right next to the teacher. He always car-ried a lot of books to class to impress the teach-ers. He'd come in just before the bell and plunk his books down hard on the desk. Dennis and I decided it would be fun to embarrass him by secretly removing the four screws which held the top of the desk to its metal base. George came in as usual, just before the bell, plunked his books down and BANG! The top of his desk and books went crashing to the floor. The class erupted in laughter. George was humiliated and had to be assigned to another desk. Dennis and I feigned surprise and innocence.

LEONA AND SANDY

I had just two girlfriends in high school, Leona and Sandy. Leona (Lee) was a short, full-bosomed Polish girl, with whom I fell madly in love during my junior year. She was blind and lived in Harvey, a southern suburb of Chicago. Talking on the phone with her after school was expensive, because it was a toll call. Love is often desperate and teenagers are often poor. So, what I would do was go to a drugstore near my house and use the pay phone. I would deposit the 35 cents for the first three minutes as required and then talk for 40 or 45 minutes more. When the operator would call back and ask to collect for the additional minutes, I would disguise my voice and announce in a muffled voice, with the telephone booth door closed: "Anyone here make a call to Harvey." Receiving no answer, I would tell the operator, "Sorry, the rascal must have already left." I don't know who wound up paying for those calls, the drugstore, Lee's dad or the phone company. How ironic that 30 years later I would go to work for Ma Bell.

My romance with Lee lasted just one semester. I walked her to class, sat next to her at school concerts and bought her presents. I remember one of her favorite recordings was Deep Purple by Paul Weston's orchestra. I saved up my nickels and dimes and walked a mile in the rain to buy it for her. Standing together in the deserted hallway outside the auditorium, we were on the verge of our first kiss, when suddenly a bunch of students appeared from out of nowhere, ruining the event.

But, alas, Lee was not a faithful sweetheart. Unbeknownst to me, she was giving her affections to another—my best friend, Dennis Mejia. When I learned of the betrayal, I confronted Dennis in the boys' bathroom. He admitted it and offered to fight me. My better judgment or cowardice prevailed. He was, after all, 30 pounds heavier and very muscular.

This double deception hurt me deeply. Friends were supposed to be loyal and sweethearts faithful. At least, that's how it was in the books I read and the radio programs I listened to. And these were my guides for morality.

After this experience I became much more cautious about showing an interest in girls. But then, in my senior year, I met Sandy, a tall, slender Jewish girl, who was one of the sighted volunteer readers for us blind students. I liked the idea of having a sighted girlfriend. Perhaps I'll be criticized for saying this, but I always knew that I would choose a sighted mate as my wife.

After Dennis' double-cross, Jack became my best friend. Jack was a year older than I, very good-looking and quite debonair around girls. I admired his smooth confidence and charm. Jack had lost his sight at age 11. So, he had full recollection of facial expressions, gestures and styles of clothing. He gave much attention to how he dressed, his posture and mannerisms. It was, in his mind, "the way you can be more accepted by sighted people." I tried to follow his example.

There was another sighted volunteer reader, named Jeanette, whom Jack liked. We decided to plan a double date and take the girls to Riverview. I would invite Sandy, and Jack would ask Jeanette.

Up to this point, aside from a few flirtatious conversations, I had only walked Sandy to her class once. So, the next day, as we stopped at her classroom door, I asked for her phone number. She gave it to me, but I was so nervous and excited that on the way back to my room, I forgot it. Feeling like a dunce, I had to ask her for it again the next day. Graciously, she gave it to me a second time.

I called her that night and invited her to go on the double date to Riverview with Jack and Jeanette. To my astonishment and joy, she accepted. In the meantime, Jack asked Jeanette, and she accepted as well.

All was set for that Saturday. Jack and I rendezvoused at his house, and then took the streetcar to Sandy's. She was eager and excited to go. Again, we took a streetcar to Jeanette's house. We had no money for taxis, and guys took girls on dates on public transportation all the time. Well, we got to Jeanette's house around 10 in the morning, and that's when our plans fell apart. Jeanette's grandmother announced that Jeanette could not go. What to do? Our choices were: I could go ahead and take Sandy to Riverview alone, but that would not show much empathy for my best friend. Jack and I could take Sandy, leaving Jeanette behind. That seemed a bit cruel. So, we decided to give up on the Riverview plan and just visit with Jeanette and her grandmother. It was a dull date. And, I never got another chance with Sandy.

LOLLAPALOOZA - HOW DO YOU SAY IT?

I didn't know I had a speech impediment until I got into high school, when some of my classmates began teasing me about it. One of the popular words of the day was "lollapalooza," which means, according to the American heritage Dictionary of the English Language, something outstanding of its kind. It was a great superlative, which could be applied to almost anything. The only problem was that I couldn't pronounce it correctly.

The "L" sound is produced differently depending on the language or dialect you are speaking. The "L" in English is known as a lateral sound. It is formed by the tip of the tongue touching the alveolar ridge and air being released laterally on one or both sides of the tongue with the front part of the tongue slightly raised towards the hard palate. The "L" in Spanish is more of an alveolar sound being produced in the region immediately behind the teeth by placing the tip of the tongue against the alveolar ridge. The French "L," by contrast, is produced further back in the mouth, with the body of the tongue pressing against the soft palate or in the uvular region. And that is how I pronounced my "L's." I didn't know I was doing it. Classmates would torment me by asking me to repeat a sentence with a lot of "L's" and then laugh mercilessly at my strange pronunciation. When I finally was able to "hear" myself by means of a tape recorder, I was able to correct the way I said lollapalooza. And my classmates had to look for another foil.

DRIVING

O ur first car was a used 1942 Ford, which Mom bought after the war. It was the last model that was manufactured before the war began, and a limited number were made. Not long after December 7, 1941, the government stopped production of autos, and ordered the car makers to start producing jeeps, tanks, and other vehicles for war. Gasoline was rationed, so was sugar and butter. The government issued ration coupons that limited how much gas or sugar or butter you could buy. Mothers carefully collected used cooking oil and lard and took it to their butcher to help the war effort. Nylon was used for making parachutes, not stockings.

We still lived on Montrose, and that Ford was the vehicle that Jimmy and I drove. Jimmy was 13 and I was 12. We decided to borrow Mom's car and take it for a drive. Jimmy didn't know much about how to shift gears and I couldn't see well enough to steer, so we decided on a team approach. Jimmy would steer and work the pedals and I would shift gears. I learned how to shift gears from Uncle Joe, who used to sit me on his lap when I was six or seven and let me move the gear shift of his '39 Chevy. We drove down the alley and around the block. We did great. No crashes, no running off the road and I think we only stalled out once. Best of all, we got back before Mom found out.

The experience left me with a longing. What would it feel like, I wondered, to sit behind the wheel and actually drive a car? Some 10 years later, I realized my dream.

NORMAN

I first met Norman when he rented the extra bedroom next to mine in the converted attic in our house on Lawndale. He called himself a cook, but he was more than that. He had a great appreciation for food–how to make it and how to enjoy it.

Norman was about 12 years my senior, about 6 ft. tall and weighed, in the best of times, around 240 pounds. Keeping down his weight was his biggest challenge. It was particularly hard for him because of how he loved to eat and what he loved to eat: ice cream shakes, French fries, steak and potatoes with lots of gravy, bacon and eggs and hot chocolate with whipped cream.

I was attending Northwestern University and working part-time at radio station WEAW in Evanston. Norman worked nights and usually got off from work around 1:00 A.M. He would come by the house, pick me up and we'd go to one of those all- night drive-in restaurants, popular back in the 50's, for coffee or hot chocolate. Fridays and Saturdays we might stay out to 3:00 or 4:00 in the morning, driving around and talking about his work, my school, food, philosophy, literature, the possibility of extra terrestrial life, religion and so much more.

It was on one of these occasions, at about 4:00 A.M., while driving along the Kennedy Expressway, that I said to Norman, "You know, I'd really like to know what it's like to drive a car."

"Okay," he said "Let's do it."

"Are you kidding?" I asked.

"No, if you're game, I am." And with that, he pulled off the freeway and came around to the passenger's side of the car. Opening the door, he said with a slight chuckle, "Slide over."

The next thing I knew I was sitting behind the steering wheel, shifting into first and easing the car off the shoulder and back on to the freeway. I felt strangely confident and calm with Norman guiding me verbally with precise staccato directions: "Left, right, right, left." It was like a surgeon giving instructions to his assistants in an operating room. Certainly the same tension was present.

I never realized just how much one has to move the steering wheel just to go straight. The slant and unevenness of the roadway requires constant correcting.

I concentrated hard, listening to Norman's voice: "Ease back on the accelerator. Now, get ready, a truck is going to pass us on the left. Move right. Hold it. Now back left. Good."

I felt and heard the 18-wheeler rumble by. "Wow, that was kinda close!" I observed.

"Just a little," he replied. "You're doing fine."

We drove along for about 15 minutes at 40 to 50 M.P.H., passing some vehicles and being passed by others. The tension mounted. My adrenalin was pumping hard. Finally, Norman asked if I had had enough. I answered in the affirmative.

"Okay." He said. I'm going to tell you to pull off on to the shoulder and stop so we can switch places. There are light poles along the road about 100 yards apart. Plenty of time to stop. When I say "now" cut right then straighten the wheel and brake. Ready?"

"Ready." I replied.

"Okay. Turn right. Now brake."

I calmly turned the wheel to the right and then back again while easing my foot on to the brake and applying slow steady pressure.

Suddenly I heard Norman yell: "Brake!"

I pushed the brake to the floor and gripped the steering wheel tensing all my muscles for the expected impact. Dirt and gravel flew around us. Mercifully the car came to a stop without colliding with a light pole.

Norman turned to me and said softly: "Well, I didn't mean quite that hard."

It was an exciting and unforgettable adventure. But that was Norman, always willing and eager to share his knowledge, his skill, and his experience with me in an effort to help me learn.

During those long late-night conversations, one of our favorite subjects was paranormal phenomena. Norman and I both strongly believed in telepathy and, in fact, we practiced it successfully with each other on a number of occasions over the years.

There was the time when I was living and attending school in Mexico City and had lost touch with Norman. I didn't know whether he was in Los Angeles, Las Vegas or Chicago. He often moved among those cities according to the season. I had come home to Chicago and had been there for just a couple of hours, when my mother and sister went out to shop for some groceries. About a half hour later, the telephone rang, and I knew it was Norman. I was right. He had run into my family at the grocery store, and they told him I had just come home. Was this coincidence? I don't think so.

On another occasion, also while I was living in Mexico, I was making plans to fly to California with my wife, Diana, and 4-year-old son, Alan, to do some job hunting. I thought how nice it would be to find Norman there. Again, it had been more than a year since I had heard from him and I had no idea where he was living at the time.

About three weeks before our departure, we received a call from his sister, Pat, who just happened to be visiting Mexico City. She confirmed that Norman was back in Los Angeles and gave us his address and telephone number. So it worked out again, that "coincidence" placed him in the right spot at the right time.

He was my friend for nearly 30 years. He loaned me money to go to college. He let me drive his car. He described movies we watched together at the drive-in. He came to my aid during a painful marriage separation. And he was not uncomfortable about my blindness; he was intrigued by it.

THE DENTIST

As a kid, I hated going to the dentist. As an adult, I still hate going to the dentist. Who doesn't? When I was around 12, my sister Eileen took me to a new dentist. He was German, and he had a German dental assistant or nurse. They talked about me in German, which was very unnerving. I've forgotten his name. I'll call him Dr. Ach du Lieber, because I remember when he looked inside my mouth he said "ach du Lieber you got bad teeth". That made me think that he was going to yank them all out.

All dentist offices smell the same, a kind of pungent, narcotic smell, and the tools of their trade haven't changed much. High speed drills still whine unnervingly as they grind away bits of our teeth, filling the air with the acrid scent of burnt enamel.

On this occasion, Dr. AchduLieber introduced me to the latest medical tool that he had added to his office for the comfort and convenience of his patients, "laughing gas." There was a hose with two small nozzles that were inserted into the patient's nostrils. Then, there was a ball that the patient held in his hand and squeezed rhythmically to cause the gas to flow into the nose. So, Dr. Achdulieber inserted the nozzles in my nose, placed the rubber ball in my hand and told me to "sqveeze da ball and open your mouth."

I began squeezing the ball and breathing in through my nose, and he began drilling. Well, apparently the gas wasn't flowing the way it was supposed to, because I winced at the pain caused by the drill.

"Vas da matter?" he asked.

"It hurts." I said.

"Vell you're not sqveezing hard enough." With that, he took the ball from my hand and gave it several strong squeezes and I was out like a light.

I dreamed of being in a German concentration camp and being interrogated by the Gestapo. "Okay, I'll talk. I'll talk." I said.

Next, I heard Dr. Achdulieber's voice coming to me from the Gestapo agent standing over me saying, "No don't talk just keep your mouth open."

I did not go back to him.

MORE BLIND THAN BEFORE

M y brother Jimmy is 18 months older than I. Frequently we expressed our sibling rivalry by fighting (sometimes it was playing and sometimes we went at it pretty seriously.) Our wrestling matches involved practicing hammerlocks, scissor grips, arm twisting, hair pulling and whatever other judo holds we knew. Being younger, I usually got the worst of it, but I never quit trying to beat him.

On one occasion, we were wrestling on our mom's bed when his right foot came up hard and the toe of his shoe hit me square in the left eye. The blood flowed down my face. I screamed in pain. One of my sisters took me to the bathroom and packed ice around the eye. It looked very ugly. Mom came home, took one look and called the doctor. He told her to bring me in right away. Back then, doctors handled emergencies right there in their office. They didn't tell their patients to go to the Emergency Room, and they would catch up with them at the hospital later, as they do today. I didn't know how bad it was, and nobody else knew either. If they did, noone said so. We climbed into the family car. Dorothy and Mom sat in the front, and I sat with Eileen in the back. Jimmy stayed behind filled with guilt and regret. I became dizzy and nauseated probably from the shock and the trauma. I threw up all over my poor sister. And, instead of scolding me she comforted me. That small show of understanding and compassion meant a lot to me then, and I have remembered it all these years.

At the doctor's office, it didn't take long for him to confirm that the eye was irreparably injured and would need to be removed. It was my left eye, the one that had better vision. Mom asked me if it was my better eye, and I lied and told her no. I didn't want her to feel anger toward my brother or pity toward me. So, off I went to the hospital to have the surgery. Back home, I followed a regimen of applying an ointment three times a day. At one point, I began noticing that the eye cavity was again taking the shape of my missing eye. I ran excitedly up to my mother and announced, "Mom, my eye is growing back."

She called the doctor who told her to have me place hot moist compresses on it. A couple hours later, the illusion dissolved in a sudden torrent of yellowish white pus. Jimmy felt really bad about the accident and offered to work extra hours at the softball stadium selling peanuts and popcorn to help pay for all the medical bills. We did not have health insurance. In fact, most families didn't. You tried to avoid going to the doctor, much less having to spend time in the hospital. If you got sick or injured, Mom would first try her home remedies. If they didn't work, she'd call the family doctor who would recommend something over the phone or she'd take us to his office for a more complete exam. If it was more serious and we were too sick for the trip to the doctor's office, the doctor would make a house call to the patient's home and prescribe treatment. That would be unheard of today where doctors try to schedule four to five patients an hour to maximize their efficiency and six-figure incomes.

I was out of school for more than a month. I was surprised and thrilled when a group of my high school classmates came by to visit. They brought me an album of Spike Jones. He was absolutely my most favorite band leader. I loved the humorous parodies he did on popular songs and the synchronized sound effects which blended in so perfectly to the changed lyrics. Several years later, I had the chance to attend a live performance of Spike and his City Slickers and to witness the water squirting out of the trumpets and other mad antics of his wacky wacketeers.

THE HOUSE ON LAWNDALE

During my recovery time, we moved. Mom had scraped and saved enough to purchase our own home. It was a two-story two-flat with a converted attic, at 4330 N. Lawndale Avenue, a half block south of Montrose. She rented out the first floor flat and the front bedroom to help pay the mortgage. The girls, Dorothy and Eileen both worked and helped contribute to the family budget. Up in the attic, which had two bedrooms, Jim and I shared one and Mom occupied the other.

We moved to Lawndale during my sophomore year of high school in the spring of 1948. I kept the tradition of my Uncle Joe and remained a loyal White Sox fan during all the years I lived in Chicago. Sometimes I had to go to extreme lengths to "listen" to the games. In the early 1950's, with the advent of television, they stopped broadcasting the White Sox night games on radio. Since our family could not yet afford a TV, I would walk to the corner tavern, buy a quart bottle of root beer (I was under 21), and watch (listen to) Jack Brickhouse describe the games on television.

MY LOYAL COMPANION

Tasha was a beautiful black Doberman Pincer and became my loyal companion when I was a month short of 16. She gave me a sense of self-confidence and independence that remained with me long after she departed.

Some people think if a blind person has a guide dog, all he needs to do is tell the dog "Take me to the supermarket." And the dog will lead him to the bus stop, select the right bus to board and bark twice when it's time to get off. Of course, it's not quite that simple. I had to know where I was going and give clear directions to the dog.

Larry, at age 16, with his brand-new guide dog Tasha, in front of house on Lawndale.

I received my guide dog from a guide dog school in Detroit, Michigan called Pathfinder. This means that Tasha was not a "Seeing Eye" dog but a "Pathfinder" dog. This is a common mistake many people make, referring to all dog guides as "Seeing Eye" dogs. There are around a dozen different dog guide schools in the U.S. today. "Seeing Eye" is located in Morristown, New Jersey and was the first guide dog school. The Pathfinder school, where I obtained my dog, no longer exists.

I remember feeling excited, nervous and a little scared. I didn't know what it meant to have a dog guide. I was told it would help me become more independent, give me more freedom. That sounded pretty good to a 15-year-old. More freedom and independence. Isn't that what all teenagers want?

What I soon found out, was that it also meant more responsibility. Bathing, brushing, feeding, exercising, getting up, sometimes at the crack of dawn, in the middle of a Chicago winter, to let "the puppy" out.

The instructors at the Pathfinder Dog Guide School were excellent. They emphasized that we, the handlers, must always be in control, and not the dog. They told us, "You have to give the dog a clear command to go forward, after stopping at an intersection. You must tell it when and where to turn. You must know where you are and where you are going."

There were three of us, and our dogs, who shared a room at the school. We were to teach them to sleep on the floor next to our beds. One night I had a terrible nightmare. I dreamt I was being held down by a psychotic murderer who was about to cut my throat. Try as I might, I could not move my arms up to protect myself. I felt a tremendous pressure upon my chest. My heart was pounding, and I tried to scream, but nothing came out. Finally, using every last ounce of strength remaining, I dug my elbows into the bed and pushed myself up into a sitting position, throwing a sleeping Tasha off my chest and onto the floor.

The dogs we received were only partially house-broken, which meant we were responsible for cleaning up any messes they made and for correcting them for their misbehavior. Strangely, I didn't mind. After all, if this pooch was going to help me have more freedom, the least I could do was to help her learn a few house manners.

Tasha was a quick learner. During the course of our training, we learned to cross streets together, to get on and off street cars, to ride escalators, and to go through revolving doors (a very tricky business). Normally, the dog guide walks on the left side. However, to go through a revolving door, because the space is wider on the right, I had to quickly switch the dog over to the right side as I went through, always waiting for the door to stop moving before I entered.

By the time we completed our three weeks of training, I felt ready to go anywhere, any time with Tasha. As I rode the train back to Chicago, I felt a lot older, more self-reliant. It was a good feeling and a sobering one too. My childhood days were over. Yes, it was going to be hard to break the news to my mom that her baby boy had grown up.

Back home, Tasha was quickly accepted by my mother and sister as a new member of our family. My mom watched apprehensively, at first, as Tasha and I moved swiftly down the sidewalk, zigzagging around startled children on tricycles and gawking neighbors, on our way to catch the bus. After a couple of weeks though, Mom began to relax, realizing that this canine companion was a wonderful guide and that I was enjoying my new-found independence.

That fall I began my studies at Wright Jr. College (now called Wilbur Wright Community College). Tasha was a huge hit with the girls, and she was a remarkable classroom critic. If an instructor's lecture droned on too long to suit her, she would lift her head, open her mouth wide and exhale a loud and resonant yawn. Some of my classmates accused me of teaching Tasha to yawn on command. I plead the fifth.

But Tasha had another social custom that was much more embarrassing. Without sound or warning, she would suddenly release into the air the foulest smelling odor you can imagine, and she did this sometimes just as I was saying goodnight to my date and hoping for a farewell kiss. Few of my friends believed me when I told them it was my dog, and not me, who was the guilty party. But her elegant beauty and proud bearing did help me to be introduced to many an admiring coed. So I had to forgive her for her occasional lack of social grace.

The Pathfinder trainers emphasized to us that as soon as we put the harness on our dogs, it meant that they were working dogs and not pets. We were a working team. They told us that it was serious stuff, that we literally were putting our lives in our dog's hands, er' paws.

It also meant that we had to guard against other people, friends and strangers alike, from feeding, petting or otherwise distracting our dog guides while working. It is, I know, a tremendous temptation to want to pet a dog guide. But, before you do, ask yourself: "If the person was being guided by their spouse, would you have the same temptation?" Well, maybe you would, but you had better not carry it out.

Dobermans have a menacing look and a fearsome reputation. Many times I would be asked by strangers: "Will she bite?" And I'd quietly reply, "only on command, only on command."

Tasha was 29 inches tall at the shoulder, weighed about 57 lbs and was all muscle. She loved to take long, brisk walks. All I needed to do was turn the door knob of the closet where her harness and leash were kept and, like a shot, she'd be down the stairs from the converted attic, where both of us slept, and ready to go.

Our house on Lawndale Avenue had two walkways, one to the front steps and the other to the backyard. Remarkably, Tasha was able to learn to respond to my verbal commands "front" or "back," correctly every time. It was really amazing how many words she did know.

We did a lot of walking together, in 100 degree plus heat, in blizzards and in thunderstorms. Thunder though, was Tasha's nemesis. She hated all loud noises–firecrackers, jackhammers, sirens. But thunder really frightened her the most. If we were out walking, and it started to thunder, she would strongly suggest that we slip in to the nearest building. If we were at home, she would go hide in a dark corner upstairs in the attic. I could never get her to overcome this fear.

One of the saddest days of my life was when Tasha became ill and had to be taken to the vet to be put to sleep. I was not brave enough to be present. She placed her gentle trusting face against my leg, and I rubbed, for the last time, those elegantly pointed ears (the left one slightly drooping as always). She uttered that strange kind of purring sound of satisfaction which she always did when I rubbed her ears. And then, we said good-bye. I was 24 at the time, and I cried.

For eight wonderful years she was my trusted guide, my faithful companion, my best friend.

AMAZING GRACE

I met her at the Chicago Lighthouse for the Blind. It was the summer after my freshman year at Wright Jr. College. I'd gone back to the Lighthouse to work on the assembly line to earn some money and stay busy during summer vacation. The work was boring, repetitive and paid just 50 cents an hour. But, because there were a bunch of my friends also working there, it was fun. We used our meager wages to organize beach parties along Lake Michigan, picnics in the forest preserves, Sunday horseback rides and other such fun activities.

Grace was a tall, slender, quite pretty girl of Irish descent. She wore her hair long and loose which I loved. She was considered a high partial, which meant that though she was legally blind, she had good travel vision and did not need or use a white cane.

She became my girlfriend almost immediately. Like me, she loved to roller-skate, and we went to many roller-skating parties with her church and at the local roller rink on Broadway. She was agreeable to go wherever I suggested, doing whatever I wanted. Her mother had died several years earlier, and her older sister was married. So, Grace lived at home with her dad and took care of him. She was an experienced housekeeper and excellent cook.

She invited me over for sumptuous Sunday dinners on a couple of occasions. The first time, not knowing that she was going to cook for me, I ate a full dinner at home before going. When I got to Grace's, I wasn't hungry, but there it was, a beautiful pot roast with baked potato and string beans waiting to be devoured. I couldn't disappoint her, so I loosened my belt and forced it down into my complaining tummy. Fortunately, I was able to put off eating the home made hot apple pie until later on.

Grace was an amazing girl and too good for me. She gave me presents, was always eager to see me, never argued, didn't smoke or drink or swear. She was strongly religious, Presbyterian, I think, and wanted nothing more than to be some fellow's loving and devoted wife.

I have to confess that I didn't have the same feelings toward her, and I didn't treat her all that well. I told her that I didn't like the name Grace, so she offered to let me call her by her middle name, Lynn. When she went to her church camp the next summer, she wrote to me and signed the letters, "Love, Lynn." She was willing to mold herself into the person I wanted her to be. But that was not what I wanted. At the tender age of 18, I was not ready for marriage, and I certainly didn't want a partner who would be totally submissive to my every wish and whim.

We had been going together for a little over a year when I decided that it was time to break it off. I remember we were in her bedroom, sitting on her bed. Her dad was in the living-room. I said to her: "I think we should stop seeing each other for a while."

She started to cry and then began reading to me a love letter that she had written but never sent, telling me of her undying love and adoration.

I felt like such a cad. This lovely, sweet, kind-hearted girl was pouring out her heart and soul to me, and all I could think about was, how can I get away from here.

It was the first time that I had so completely won and then broken the heart of a young maiden. A year and a half later, the tables would be turned, and I would understand the pain and disappoint-ment that I had caused this sweet girl.

TELLING TIME

I'd learned how to tell time in school from a clock face made out of cardboard and the hands fastened to it with a metal eye which allowed the hands to move easily all the way around. It was fun, but I wanted to be able to do it with a real clock. So, I got my mom to let me remove the glass from a cheap wind-up alarm clock, and it became my symbol of independence. I carried it with me whenever I could. It felt great to know what time it was without having to ask anyone. I felt really proud of my ability to tell time independently.

Then, one day, Mom told me there was a group of Kiwanis members on the south side who wanted to meet me. She didn't say why, and I was reluc-tant to go. But I relented and grabbed my special clock to take along. After about an hour and a half streetcar and bus ride we arrived. There were four or five gentlemen waiting for us, very excited. To my complete surprise, they presented me with an elegant Gotham braille wristwatch with a stainless steel cover. I had never felt a braille watch before. It was so small compared to my clock. I wasn't sure I could read the time that well. My hesitancy and lack of enthusiasm no doubt was a disappointment to them.

I learned to use that watch, to love it and relied on it for 7 years until it was stolen from me in Mexico. I continue to use braille watches, preferring them over talking watches. I think they are much more discrete. If I'm in a meeting with the boss or a customer, and want to know how long before lunch, I don't want some automated voice embarrassing me by announcing the time.

ON HORSEBACK

In our early 20's a number of us visually impaired guys and girls became interested in horse-back riding. For $3.50 we could do a two-hour breakfast ride on Saturday or Sunday morning. The riding stable was at the entrance to the forest preserve at the end of Milwaukee Avenue. There were seven or eight of us. Some, like Paul and Dennis (not the Dennis from high school who had stolen my girl friend, but Dennis Rainsford) had pretty good vision. Others of us like Wanda, Jack and I, were totally blind. We tried to get the same horses each week, so they would know us and we would know them.

My favorite was a beautiful black gelding named Midnight. On a particular Sunday the ride started off well. We trotted along the bridal path between the trees. Paul, Wanda and Jim with our guide in the lead, then Bill, Dennis and Joan. I was last, deliberately. I thought it would be fun to let the others get a good lead and then put Midnight into a gallop and catch up in a cloud of dust. Well, what happened instead was that Midnight tripped over a branch or root or something and fell caplunk on his belly. I wasn't sure what to do. I thought if I got off him, it might be easier for him to get up. That is, if he hadn't broken a leg. So I climbed off and encouraged him to stand up, which he did, and promptly trotted off. I'd forgotten to hold on to his reins. Oh my God, what'll I do if he leaves me here in the middle of the forest preserve? But he didn't go far. I could hear him munching on some grass about 30 feet away. Slowly I approached him, speaking softly to him all the while. It was as if he were waiting for me. I found the reins and mounted. I hesitated wondering, which way do we go? Then I thought well, he's been doing this ride often enough, he ought to know which way is home. So, I'll just leave it up to him. "Let's go, Midnight," I said. And off we went. But instead of taking the trail, he decided to take a shortcut through the woods. Branches slapped at me from every side, scratching and scraping my face and arms. It was a wild ride, but we quickly caught up to the group. The guide looked at me and asked what had happened. I told him. He recommended that I stick with the group from then on, adding that I looked like I had been in a fight with three angry tomcats.

DENNIS AND PAUL

Two of my good buddies during my college years and beyond were Dennis Rainsford and Paul Kish. We met in Boy Scouts and remained friends until their untimely deaths some 20 years later. In grammar school and high school they attended what was called sight-saving class. This meant that they were legally blind but had sufficient vision to be able to read large print and travel without a cane or dog guide. For a kid who is partially sighted, it's like living in limbo. You're not blind enough for people to make allowances for your visual impairment, and you're not sighted enough to do everything a fully sighted person can do. But they tried.

I love to tell one story about Dennis and Paul. Paul decided that he wanted to own a car. They walked into a used car lot and picked out a ten-year-old jalopy which the salesman was willing to let Paul have for just $50 bucks, no questions asked. Neither Paul nor Dennis had a driver's license, but that didn't matter. The salesman was happy to make the sale. So, off they went. Well, the story goes, according to Dennis, they drove along for about ten or twelve blocks when Paul decided to make a turn. Dennis tried to object, saying that he didn't think there was a street there to turn on. But Paul was confident there was, and so he turned, right into a vacant lot and down into a small ravine. Luckily, neither was hurt. What to do? To get the car back up out of the ditch would prove both expensive and embarrassing. So, they decided to do the next best thing, and leave it there. Thus, it became someone else's trash or treasure.

Neither Paul nor Dennis ever carried a white cane. To do so, they said, would make them appear blind. Even today, I know many people, most of them seniors who have lost vision due to macular degeneration, glaucoma or diabetic retinopathy, who steadfastly refuse to carry a white cane because, in their mind, it labels them as blind. They prefer to be guided by a sighted spouse or friend, not realizing or admitting that this limits their independence even more.

WRIGHT COLLEGE

J immy and I started at Wright Junior College the same year, because I had been skipped two half grades in grammar school. I was just 16. We had different interests and different friends. So we didn't hang out together, and hardly anyone knew that we were brothers. I was now taller than Jimmy by an inch, which meant he had to look up to me. I grew seven inches during my four years in high school and added four more during my years at college. Consequently, Jimmy began referring to me as his Big Little Brother, and I refer to him as my Little Big Brother. To this day, we often address or sign birthday cards or emails to each other with the initials LBB or BLB.

Oddly enough, during the two years we were at Wright, we had only one class, in psychology, with the same instructor, and even that class we had at different hours. Jim remembers that we both got A's.

Soon after I started at Wright, I was invited to join a fraternity. I felt really special and thrilled to be asked. It was called Mu Omega Beta (or MOB for short). It was very much of a social fraternity. Every Wednesday night there was a mixer—a beer party with one of the sororities at some local beer hall. A lot of the guys were army vets who took a brotherly interest in me and a special satisfaction in making sure that I got rides to and from all the mixers. No one seemed to notice or care that I was five years under the legal drinking age. I learned to play the chug-a-lug game like everyone else, drinking down a full bottle of beer without taking a breath.

As a pledge, I had to learn to recite the Greek alphabet, memorize the names of all the members, address them as "Sir" and do their bidding. We pledges also had to carry around a Pledge Book wherein would be recorded demerits by members who determined that we were either not sufficiently prepared with our responses to them or not courteous enough in our manner. These demerits could be erased by special acts of kindness toward a member or, more often, by submitting to a paddling, one swat for each demerit from the pledge's own paddle, at the Friday fraternity meeting.

"Hell Night" happened on a Saturday night near the end of the semester. The pledges were all blindfolded, except for me, and then driven to a deserted house out in the country owned by the parents of one of the members. Once there, we were obliged to strip naked and be subjected to several hours of physical and verbal abuse and humiliation. Our testicles were painted with Wintergreen oil. Globs of Limburger cheese were smeared across our upper lips, just under the nose, and we were fed raw garlic, we were grilled on the historical significance of "The Message to Garcia." A wrong answer or discourteous remark from a pledge resulted in that pledge being told to "Assume the position." The "position" was to bend over and grasp one's ankles and make ready to receive a swat from the paddle and say: "Thank you, sir." Failure to say "sir" earned you another swat. I remember one member, L.D. Green, who swatted me so hard, I fell over. He considered this an affront and obliged me to take another swat, down on all fours.

Why did we do this? Why did we allow it to be done? It had something to do with power and with earning the right of passage. We wanted to belong, to be accepted, and we were willing to be intimidated, humiliated and abused. My view today is that such initiation practices are cowardly, cruel, and even dangerous.

Jim Stevens was one of my frat brothers who took a special liking to me. He was a Korean War vet, about 21 and a very handsome guy. One afternoon during the Christmas/New year holiday vacation, he invited me over to his house to teach me how to play chess. With a bottle of Mogen David wine by our elbow, he patiently explained the game, what the different pieces were called and how they moved on the board. Whether it was beginner's luck or I was a quick learner or the wine dulled Jim's senses just enough, I'm not sure. But I won that game, and Jim refused to play me again, accusing me of trickery, certain that I had already known how to play.

During my second year at Wright College, I became less interested in fraternity life and more interested in theater. Acting seemed like a wonderful way to learn about natural body gestures

and spatial movement which I knew could be a real benefit to me as a blind person. The facial expressions and gestures of sighted individuals communicate a great deal of information. On the other hand, the faces and gestures of persons who have been blind all of their life, like myself, may often transmit erroneous information–frowns or smiles which have nothing to do with the conversation or may be totally devoid of any expression, thus bewildering or confusing to the observer.

And so, I took drama in my sophomore year at Wright College. The name of our drama director was Mr. Johnson, and he made me feel welcome right from the start. As we built scenery, rehearsed our lines and helped each other with makeup and costumes during class and after school, we drew very close as a group and were more caring of one another. One of my classmates was Jim Matson, a sensitive, talented student, about a year older than I. He was not bothered by my blindness; rather he was curious about it. He loved acting and encouraged me to try out for any part I was interested in. We became good friends. Sometimes when rehearsals would run late, Jim would invite me to stay over at his house which was much nearer to the college than mine. Because we were broke most of the time, we'd often hitchhike to and from school, which was a common practice among students and servicemen back then. There was little fear or apprehension on our part or on the part of motorists. We were glad to save the bus fare.

Larry and Eddie Matthews as Executioners
in the play "The Enchanted" at Wright
Jr. College in Chicago, 1953

During the first semester, Mr. Johnson chose "The Enchanted." a French comedy by Jean Giraudoux, as the play to be performed to a public audience of students, parents and friends. I tried out for the part of one of the executioners, and Eddie Matthews and I were chosen and given the part. Eddie was about a foot shorter than I, so we made for a very comic duo as we acted, danced and sang together. In one piece of business, I threw my arms out wide hitting Eddie in the chest and knocking him on his fanny. The audience loved it. Mr. Johnson invited the local newspapers to come to our opening and let them know that one of the members of his cast was blind, but he didn't say which one. He told me later with a chuckle, "They tried to figure it out but guessed wrong."

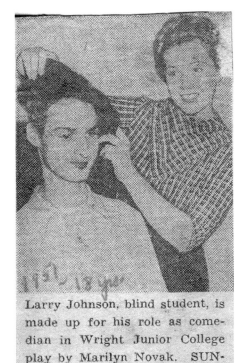

Larry Johnson, blind student, is made up for his role as comedian in Wright Junior College play by Marilyn Novak. SUN-

Larry, at 17, at Wright Jr. College, having stage makeup applied by fellow classmate Marilyn (Kim) Novak.

Ironically, one of the girls who didn't get cast for a part in the play, but who helped me with my makeup, was named Marilyn Novak. Later, she went to Hollywood, changed her name to Kim and became a big star. Our director apparently didn't recognize her hidden talents.

In the spring semester we got a new drama director and we did a play about a Pennsylvania Dutch family entitled "Papa Is All" by Patterson Greene. I played the state trooper who arrests Papa.

BLIND SERVICE

One of the major challenges for blind students attending college is finding an adequate number of readers to read aloud or record the immense amount of print materials–textbooks, literature assignments, reference materials, lecture hand-outs, etc., which college instructors love to pour out upon their hapless students. Thus, I was truly fortunate to hear about the Blind Service Association, a wonderfully helpful, local, charitable organization located in down-town Chicago.

BSA provided me with hundreds of hours of volunteer reading assistance during my college years and beyond. They also provided free canes, paper, slates and styluses (for writing), and hosted a number of free dinners and parties throughout the year, particularly around Thanksgiving and Christmas.

At any given time, there were probably 20 or more blind college students regularly taking advantage of Blind Service's volunteer reader service. During the time that I was a student, BSA's offices were on the top floor of 127 N. Dearborn. Each student and volunteer had their own small reading room with a desk and two chairs. Volunteers were scheduled for two-hour shifts—10:00 AM to 12:00 noon, 1:00 to 3:00 and 3:00 to 5:00 PM. For those students whose class schedule did not allow them to come during the day or who needed extra reading time there was also a 6:00 to 8:00 PM schedule. BSA had a small recording studio and volunteers took requests for textbooks to be recorded on thin vinyl discs which could be played by the students on their Talking Book machines provided by the National Library Service.

I had some wonderful volunteer readers at Blind Service–Winifred Healey, Jesse Garcia, Ethel Press, Elsie Baccus. Mrs. Press remained one of my readers during the entire time I used BSA's service, almost 7 years. Jesse Garcia introduced me to many of her friends in the Mexican-American community in Chicago, and when I told her that I was planning a visit to Mexico the summer of 1952, she gave me a letter of introduction to a marvelous family in Mexico City. Mrs. Healey remained a dear friend long after I finished college. She would invite me and other former students over to her home for an evening of stimulating conversation and a dish of lemon sherbet drenched with chocolate syrup.

I have wonderful memories of the hours I spent at Blind Service–of those kind, patient and dedicated volunteers, of my struggle to stay awake during long passages of boring texts and of the sometimes serious, sometimes light-hearted banter between fellow students during our breaks between reading sessions.

Some of those fellow students were female. And, several of us extended our relationships beyond just a shared cigarette in the hallway. Joan was an intelligent and seductively sexy blonde who had an excitingly sultry voice, especially when she sang the song "Temptation." We dated a few times. Once we went to a New Year's Eve party at a bar where a guy pulled out a gun. We dove under the table and stayed there until someone got the gun away from him. Scary. Joan was a lot of fun, but she was interested in marriage, and I wasn't.

Eunice was a tall, heavy-boned but strikingly attractive redhead. She had a beautiful and powerful operatic voice, but years of smoking, took their toll. She was an excellent conversationalist, a good dancer and could drink me under the table. We went on a few dates and then, after college, our paths diverged. I moved to Mexico, and she went off to New York.

Twenty years later, we met at a cross-country ski event for visually impaired persons in Minnesota. A strong bond of friendship was formed. At that time, Eunice was the disability advocate for the Mayor's office in New York City and deeply involved in the disability rights movement across the country. She motivated me to become actively involved in the movement as well. I am convinced that it was in part because of her example, her energy and her enthusiasm that I was motivated to helped found the Coalition of Texans with Disabilities, a statewide cross-disability advocacy organization which has flourished now for 30 years, and the San Antonio Independent Living Services, a local nonprofit agency which offers peer counseling, information and referral and direct services to hundreds of persons with disabilities throughout Bexar County and surrounding counties.

Later, Eunice moved to Washington D.C. to take a job with the federal government, where she continued her strong advocacy efforts on behalf of people with disabilities. During a difficult period of unemployment for me, she reached out and offered advice, assistance and valuable contacts. We remained close friends and common allies in the cause for disability rights for many years, until her death in 1999.

I was curious to find out if the Blind Service Association was still providing services to blind persons in the Chicago area. So, I recently contacted them and was delighted to learn that indeed, they continue to offer their wide range of invaluable services to hosts of blind students and adults after more than 75 years. Thank you BSA, and thank you to all the wonderful volunteers.

POMPEYO

I met Pompeyo at a Thanksgiving luncheon offered by the Blind Service Association. One of the BSA volunteer ladies approached me, and said that there was a blind man from Mexico at the luncheon and asked if I wanted to meet him, since I knew some Spanish. I said, "Sure." She took me over to meet him and his wife, Esther. Pompeyo knew very little English, so I was at a decided advantage having completed two years of Spanish in high school and another two years at Wright College, plus my three weeks in Mexico City as a tourist. Esther spoke perfect English as well as Spanish and Swedish. She was the daughter of a Swedish missionary and lived most of her adult life in Mexico. Pompeyo was short, maybe 5' 6", quite chunky and slow in his movements and his speech. I nicknamed him the "Fat Turtle" (Tortugordo). He didn't mind it; in fact he thought it rather funny.

I learned that he was a very accomplished musician and that he loved to drink beer. We spent a lot of time together, at his small apartment, listening to records, talking and enjoying Esther's delicious cooking.

Pompeyo introduced me to Nellie de Tejeda, the owner of El Jarocho Restaurant, who became one of the sponsors of my radio show. She served one special dish that I've not found anywhere else, baby spareribs cooked with kidney beans. Absolutely delicious.

I visited Pompeyo at some of the clubs and bars where he played organ, piano or keyboard. He introduced me to drug addicts, ladies of the night and more than a couple of shady characters. I remember, one evening we were with his friend Max and went to some guy's apartment to share a few beers. Suddenly the guy pulls out a gun and announces that he doesn't like "gringos", Americans. Since I am the only "gringo" in the bunch, I get quite nervous. Max and Pompeyo tell the guy to put the gun down and just have another beer. We talk a bit more as he plays with the gun in his lap. At last, he gets up and heads for the kitchen to get himself another cold one. That's when Max, Pompeyo and I dash down the two flights of stairs to the street in record time with the guy yelling at us from above. Fortunately, no shots are fired. We don't stop running till we turn the corner, and whatever buzz we had from the beers is long gone.

One extremely annoying habit of Pompeyo's was his never being on time. He was always late, not a little late but a lot late. If we agreed to meet somewhere at 3 in the afternoon, he might show up at 4:30 or 5:00 P.M. It would drive me crazy. One time I decided to teach him a lesson. I told him I would meet him at 2:00 and deliberately got there at 4:00. He wasn't there. I thought, oh my gosh, maybe he came and left already. As I was thinking about what to do, the next bus pulled up and off steps Pompeyo unperturbed. Again, I was too early.

On one occasion, when Esther was back in Mexico visiting her folks and Pompeyo was alone in the apartment, he told me that his friend Max had brought over a girl who was an addict and that he wanted to borrow Pompeyo's place to help her go cold turkey. Pompeyo was uncomfortable with the idea and asked me to call the apartment and pretend I was with Western Union and had a message from Pompeyo's father-in-law saying he was arriving the next day. I made the call, and Max and the girl were forced to leave. I felt badly thinking later, maybe Pompeyo should have allowed them to stay and maybe she would have kicked the habit.

Pompeyo's favorite beer was Heineken's, imported from Holland. We loved drinking beer while eating raw onions and French fries. Oh my, the gas that this combination produces. Noone would want to be in the same room with us.

Suffice to say, I learned a lot of Spanish playing around with Pompeyo, many words and phrases that are not in any academic textbooks. It prepared me well for my subsequent trips back to Mexico.

NORTHWESTERN UNIVERSITY

In the fall of 1952, I enrolled in the School of Speech at Northwestern University to study radio broadcasting. Shortly after registering, I was summoned to the Dean's office. His purpose was to persuade me to choose a career other than radio. He saw too many obstacles, too many problems for a blind person to have to overcome.

He began by explaining that in broadcasting it was essential to be able to tell time to the second. I showed him my special pocket watch which opened so I could feel the secondhand.

"Okay," he said. "You're also going to have to be able to read commercials and the news". I explained those things could be done using braille.

He concluded by saying "Well, Larry, there are going to be many obstacles you'll face as a blind person, if you insist on entering this profession".

I realized he was right. But the problems, I understood, would not be due to my physical blindness so much as they would be due to the attitudes of sighted people, like him. I'm glad that he was so honest with me. Partly because of his opposition and doubts, I became more determined than ever to succeed.

The main campus of Northwestern University is a cluster of buildings which lie along the jagged shoreline of Lake Michigan in Evanston, a northern suburb of Chicago. I commuted to class each day, which meant a 30 min. bus ride to Broadway, a block and a half walk north to Wilson Avenue to catch the El, a change of trains at Howard Street and then a 5 block walk to the campus from where I left the El. Not a difficult journey for my guide dog Tasha and me when the weather was mild, but, such a walk during mid January could be frigidly numbing, with the wind blowing off the lake and the temperature hovering around zero.

I remember arriving once to my 8:00 AM radio announcing class and asking the professor if he could schedule me last to read the commercials we were assigned to read aloud, because my fingers were so frozen that I couldn't feel the braille dots on the page. His roguish reply drew raucous laughter from my classmates, "I thought I'd heard all the excuses until yours."

Evanston also being a chapter headquarters of the WCTU, the Woman's Christian Temperance Union, meant that there were no bars or liquor stores in town. Students had to drive a mile and a half to Howard Street, the city limits, to stock up on rum and vodka and gin for the Friday and Saturday night frat and sorority parties. Since I did not live on campus, I was not invited to join a fraternity, but I did almost become a member of a sorority.

The Delta Gamma Sorority had, at that time, as one of its national commitments, the providing of reader assistance to blind or visually impaired college students. I was lucky enough to be the only blind student on the NU campus which meant that I had the entire DG House as my personal pool of volunteer readers. Whether they were accompanying me to the library to look up and dictate reference materials or reading chapters from texts on social psychology in the sorority house, they were always very gracious, distractingly lovely and eager to help. I shall not forget their kindness.

Several months before I began classes at Northwestern, I had a dream. I was standing in a large room in front of a counter next to a young woman whose name somehow I knew to be Shirley Schubert. I turned to her and asked, "Is it open or closed"? Then I woke up. I didn't know anyone named Shirley Schubert. I did know a girl named Jean Schubert, and I knew several girls named Shirley. So, I concluded I must have simply merged the names. But the question: "Is it open or closed," had no meaning for me.

Shortly after enrolling at Northwestern and learning about Delta Gamma's special program of reader assistance to blind college students, I met a girl named Shirley Schubert. We walked to the library to check out some reference materials. On the way, she explained to me that some books could be taken out while others you had to use there in the library. "How do you know which is which" I asked. "It's simple". She said. "You just ask if it's on open or closed reserved"?

A few minutes later I was standing in front of a counter, turning to Shirley as she received the book we'd requested from the librarian and asking her, "Is it open or closed?" My dream returned, and I felt goose bumps all over.

Northwestern had a small, low-power, on-campus FM radio station, WNUR. It was primarily for students in the radio and drama departments to hone their skills. In the spring quarter of 1958, the station program director asked me if I would be interested in hosting "Box Seat", a weekly show on opera. Well, opera was not something I knew much about or particularly enjoyed, but it was a chance to be on the radio. I said, "Sure." The program's format consisted of playing recorded selections from a different opera each week and reading excerpts from its libretto. To prepare, I'd go to the library with one of my readers and have her dictate the story line and commentary from the record album, which I'd take down in braille. Then I'd choose and time the selections I planned to play and rewrite my script to be read on the air. The preparation took twice as much time as doing the show, which is about the average. It was fun and I learned a lot about opera.

When I returned to classes in the fall for my senior year, the station manager had come up with a new program idea for me–hosting an interview show, with some of the international students attending Northwestern, as my guests. It was a terrific idea. Talking with those students, I learned so much about their customs and cultures. The show was called: "We, the Strangers."

Typically, a day or so before the show, I would meet with the student I planned to interview. I'd ask them all kinds of questions about their country, culture, customs and cuisine. I'd take my notes in braille . Then they would meet me at the studio, and we'd do the interview live. I would keep track of the time using my Ingersol pocket watch, whose glass I had removed and replaced with a hinged metal cover. It was amazingly accurate. That faithful, old wind-up watch, which cost me just one dollar, served me well in my career for almost 20 years.

I met and interviewed students from dozens of nations, from all over the world. I recall meeting and interviewing one lovely graduate student from Japan. She was fascinating to talk with. It was the first time I had ever met anyone from Japan. Leaving the studio at 7:30 P.M., after the show, we were strolling across campus when she casually mentioned, "Today is my birthday."

"Really?" I replied. "How are you going to celebrate it?"

"Oh, I don't know." she said. "I don't have any plans".

Hmmm. Was this an opening for me to invite her out? So tempting, except, I already had a date for that evening with a girl from Bolivia to go roller-skating. Could I, should I, break my date with her and do instead the gallant thing by inviting this lovely, lonely lady from Japan to spend her birthday with me? She might be very....grateful. But alas, Silvia was waiting for me, and a gentleman does not disappoint a lady. So, I wished Matsuko a happy birthday and said good-night, pondering over what might have been.

The Delta Gamma House held a fund-raising dance each Valentine's Day, and as their special protégé, I was supposed to attend. I balked, saying that I didn't have anyone to go with. No problem they replied, we'll fix you up, and so they did. My date was a tall, lovely brunette named Ginger, from another sorority across the quadrangle. I am not a great dancer, but neither was Ginger, so we were a good match. I even dated her a few times afterward.

The DG girls got used to me showing up at any time of the day and on any day of the week, either to be read to or to pick up a tape recording of some material that they had made for me. One Saturday morning I asked Norman to drive me to the sorority house to pick up a textbook I had left there the day before. We arrived around 10:00 AM. One of the sisters let us in and asked us to wait while she went to find the sister who had my book. As we sat there in the hallway, some of the girls strolled in to say hello. Since it was Saturday, and they knew I couldn't see them, some of them came in not fully dressed, still in their pajamas or wearing slips. Norman was quietly observing the scene. Suddenly, pointing at Norman, one of the girls shrieked "Oh my god, he can see." There was a mass exodus. Norman told me to bring him back anytime I wanted.

The "Hut" was an off-campus sandwich shop where a lot of us students hung out. It was owned by Hank, a big burly man with a booming voice and a friendly smile. His bologna sandwiches were absolutely the best. Half inch thick slices of bologna on Jewish rye with plenty of mustard and a big kosher pickle on the side. There were times, though, when we couldn't afford any of Hank's delicious deli creations. So, we'd sit together at a booth, ask for a couple of cups of hot water and a package of crackers, pour catsup in the hot water, add some salt and pepper and presto, tomato soup. Or we'd bring along our own tea bag, drop it in the hot water, add sugar and cream and buy a couple of bagels to share.

Hank was very understanding in our periods of poverty and never begrudged us the hot water or the other fixings to make our meager lunches.

TWICE TWENTY ONE

B y my late teens, birthdays were pretty unimportant to me and rarely celebrated. Just my sister Eileen and I were at home. Dorothy was married and Jim had joined the Army. So, when August came around and my 20th birthday, I expected to spend the evening quietly at home. In another week I would be back at Northwestern to start my senior year.

It was hot and muggy, as most August evenings are in Chicago. I was lying in bed listening to the radio, when my mom called me and asked me to go out in the backyard and take down the laundry from the clothesline. There were no electric clothes dryers back then, and if there were, we didn't have one. So, after sudsing and rinsing the family laundry in our Bendix washing machine, Mom would load it all up in a huge wicker laundry basket, carry it down the stairs to the backyard and hang each item on one of several clotheslines strung between the house and the garage. My job, when I was available, was to take the clothes down, put them in the basket, collect all the clothespins in a cloth bag that hung around my waist and carry the basket back upstairs so Mom could sort, fold and put it all away. Of course, the basket of dry laundry was much lighter, but it still was a chore I didn't find much pleasure in.

I pretended at first not to hear, but she called again. "Go out in the backyard and bring me in the laundry."

Grudgingly I assented. "Okay." Slowly I descended the stairs from my bedroom in the attic, made my way past the dining-room table, through the kitchen and to the back porch where Mom kept the laundry basket. "Why couldn't it wait until tomorrow? It's not going to rain." I said.

"No. I need the clothes tonight, so I can fold them and put them away." She answered.

I picked up the laundry basket and clothespin bag and started down the stairs to the back yard, muttering as I went. I placed the basket at the foot of the stairs and began walking slowly through the grass with my hands stretched above my head feeling for the first clothesline. "Where the heck is it?" I mumbled with annoyance.

"Surprise!" A chorus of voices shouted. And then: "Happy birthday to you. Happy birthday to you. Happy birthday old Larry. Happy birthday to you."

"What's going on?" I said.

"Well, it's your birthday, and we came to have a party."

I was dumbstruck and embarrassed, with my clothespin bag hanging around my waist. Then, Mom came down and said: "I'll take that from you. Have fun with your friends."

Many of them were there–Dennis and Paul, Jim, Wanda, Eunice, Joan, Bill, Bob, Jack. I can't remember all who were there. Mom saw to it that we had lots to eat. Then the gang said: "Come on, let's go to the corner tavern and buy you a drink to celebrate."

"But I'm only 20." I said.

"Don't worry. You're with us." All of them were at least a year older than I. So, off we went to the tavern on the corner of Lawndale and Montrose, the same tavern where I went to listen to the White Sox games on television and drink my quart of root beer.

As we entered the establishment my friends joyously and scandalously proclaimed: "It's Larry's birthday, Larry's birthday, and we're here to help him celebrate." Shep, the bartender, knew me well, but didn't know exactly how old I was. Caught up by the raucous exuberance of my friends, he assumed that we must be celebrating my 21st birthday. He even bought me a drink. Back then, bartenders at neighborhood taverns were not so careful about checking ID's, and the law was not as sternly enforced. We played a few songs on the jukebox, had a couple more drinks and decided to move our party on. It was a terrific evening–a birthday to remember.

Since Shep now thought I was 21, I had to make sure to perpetuate the myth. Two or three times a week I would stop by for a glass of beer and maybe a shot of bourbon. This combination, known as a Boilermaker really hits the spot on a cold December evening. I kept up the deception for a whole year. And then, on my birthday, my real 21st birthday, I quietly entered the tavern and sat at the bar. When Shep asked: "What'll it be?"

I said softly, "Your choice. Today's my birthday. I'm 21."

"What? I thought you were 21 last year."

"Well, I'm 21 for the second time. This time for real."

RAQUEL

I met her at a function of the PanAmerican Club. She was lovely, poised, intelligent. I was immediately attracted to her, and I asked her out, to a concert. She said she would have to bring along her cousin, Josefina, because her family would not allow her to go on a date alone. I showed my annoyance but agreed. I told myself that I had to learn and accept the customs of other cultures.

Raquel's family was from Puerto Rico, and she was the only daughter which, in part, was why her parents were so protective. One date led to another. Soon I earned the family's trust, and Raquel and I were permitted to go out without the need of a chaperone. We went to the movies or out for pizza.

For her birthday I took her dancing to the Aragon Ballroom, back then a very popular and elegant venue which featured live orchestras. I gave her a corsage and a love poem in Spanish by Amado Nervo. It was a very romantic evening. I was deeply in love. But I sensed that Raquel's feelings for me were not as strong as mine for her.

We had been going together for just over a year, and I believed that one day we would be married. Raquel had a good job working as an x-ray technician, while I, on the other hand, was still in college and facing an uncertain career future. We were having supper at our favorite Italian restaurant when suddenly she turned to me and said in her quiet sweet voice: "I need to stop seeing you."

"What? Why?" I stammered.

"My parents do not approve. They do not want me to marry an American boy. I am sorry. I am very fond of you, but I must do what my parents say."

Shock and disbelief left me speechless. Was I hearing her right? Her parents objected to my being an American? I knew of instances of prejudice by Americans toward Puerto Ricans. But, I had never ever imagined it could be the other way around.

"It can't be." I protested. "I love you." I sobbed.

"I'm sorry" she said softly. And there was nothing more to say. I held her tightly, for the last time, and I cried.

How cunningly cruel and capricious Cupid can be! A year and a half earlier I was the one inflicting the pain of rejection on one who loved me. Tonight, I am made to feel what surely she must have felt–the bitter grief of loss, the loneliness and emptiness of a dream unfulfilled, the agony of helplessness.

I walked her home in silence. Turning away from Raquel's door, I walked the five miles home in a daze, carelessly crossing streets, oblivious to the honking horns and squealing brakes, praying that my misery and my young life might be swiftly and mercifully ended. But my guardian angels were on the job, and I survived.

About three months later, once I had regained my senses, to some degree at least, I decided to call Raquel to see how she was doing. She invited me to dinner at her home, to meet her new boy friend. On arriving I was introduced to him–an American.

What she had told me had been a lie. I never learned or asked about the real reason for her decision to break off our relationship. Perhaps it was my blindness. Perhaps it was my not having a full-time job. Perhaps it was both, or perhaps it was neither. It didn't really matter. She had wanted it to end, and she had lied. The pain was deep, and it took time, a long time, to forget.

LA FIESTA

My first chance to break into commercial radio came when I was a senior at Northwestern. A friend told me about a Evanston AM/FM radio station that was willing to make air time available to an eager and enterprising NU radio major to produce a program and sell advertising. I jumped at the chance, met the owner, Edward A. Wheeler, (same initials as the call letters of the station, WEAW) and he gave me a 30 minute block of time on Saturday afternoon.

Because of my strong and continued interest in the language, culture and history of Mexico and Latin America, I decided to produce a program of Latin American music. I called it "La Fiesta." My first act was to persuade the owner of Casa Panamericana, a record store in Chicago on S. Halsted that specialized in music of Spain and Latin America, to loan me records for my show. In exchange, I offered to read a short 20 sec. spot announcement about his store on my program. It worked really great all throughout the three years that I did the show. He gave me a lot of deejay promotional copies of 45 and 78 RPM records and sold me albums at a big discount. In my library today, 50 years later, I still have many of those wonderful old recordings by unforgettable artists such as Jorge Negrete, Pedro Vargas, Pedro Infante, Tona la Negra, Los Panchos and Los Tres Diamantes. This is music that breathed romance, whose melodies and lyrics were crafted by composers who knew how to touch the hearts and souls of those in love.

The way I was to make money from my program was by selling advertising. I earned a commission on every sponsor I secured. My first week, Mr. Wheeler gave me a list of current advertisers on the station. In my naiveté, I thought he was being helpful to me, so I began contacting these businesses to ask them to sponsor my show. Well, I got chewed out big time. This, I was told, is the list of businesses I was not to contact. My first lesson in commercial radio.

So, I began prospecting for my own advertisers. During my three years with WEAW, I was able to get a good number of sponsors—a travel agency, a couple of dance studios, a mambo club, a driving school and a really fine Mexican restaurant on N. Wabash called El Jarocho. I used to eat there often and became good friends with the owner. I didn't make a lot of money, but I loved being on radio. From time to time I'd get calls at the station or letters from listeners, and that made the economic struggle more worth while.

I would come in and do my show live on AM. At which time it would be recorded and replayed on FM later that day. Getting to the station meant taking the Montrose Avenue bus to Broadway, catching the El to Evanston and then walking about four blocks to the station. It was a good 40 minute trek each way.

I always took great pride in being prepared for my program, selecting what music I would play and writing out the comments I wanted to share. There was one show I did, however, that I do not remember doing.

The night before, I went out bar hopping with my buddy, Dennis Rainsford. Dennis was a big, tall, Irish kid with a happy-go-lucky disposition and always ready to share a beer or two. Because Dennis was partially sighted, he was in charge of guiding us from neighborhood bar to neighborhood bar. Somewhere around midnight we had a silly disagreement and parted ways. So, now I was left to find my way home. I counted what I thought were the right number of streets, turned right on what I thought to be Lawndale, my street, and weaved my way down the block to my house. I climbed the stairs to my porch, except it wasn't my porch. Some guy opened the upstairs window and told me to get the hell off his porch. I went back down the steps to the sidewalk. Now, totally confused and very drunk, I laid down on the sidewalk and went to sleep.

The next thing I heard was a policeman's voice telling me to get up. He asked me where I lived. It took three times for me to say my address, before he could understand my thick-tongued drunken slur. Incredibly he helped me into his patrol car and drove me home. I thanked him and staggered my way up the front steps into the house and climbed the stairs up to my attic bedroom where I collapsed.

My next memory was waking up Saturday afternoon and being mortified at having missed doing my show. I called the station to talk to the on-duty announcer to ask what he had done to fill my 30 minute time slot. He laughed and said: "Are you kidding me? You were here, and you did a great show. In fact, after you left, there were a number of calls from listeners and from a prospective advertiser."

I didn't remember any of it. I thought, well, if that's the secret to doing a good program, maybe I need to get drunk more often.

ROOMERS

To help pay the bills, Mom rented out the front bedroom. We had a lot of very unusual, yet interesting guests. There was Sam, a mild-mannered, middle-aged man who was in the process of getting a divorce. He managed an industrial cafeteria for a company on the near north side of Chicago. We became good friends. He even got me a job at his place for one week during the summer as a dishwasher.

Sam wanted to get away for a few days. He suggested that we drive up to Wisconsin and rent a cabin near a lake. It sounded great to me. I was out of school for the summer and had no other vacation plans.

It was a lovely little spot with lots of pine trees. The lake at the edge of which our cozy little cabin sat, was about 3/4 miles wide and reportedly full of fish. Sam had borrowed a small outboard motor from a friend, and we were able to rent a boat at the pier. Bright and early the next morning, we loaded our fishing rods, bait and beer into the boat and off we chugged to the middle of the lake. The first hour passed quite uneventfully. No fish. Not even a tiny bite. But the beer was cold and the breeze refreshing. Halfway into the second hour, the breeze became a strong wind. As is often the case on those northern Wisconsin lakes, the waters suddenly became very choppy. We decided it would be prudent to head for shore and try our luck the following day.

Sam hit the switch of the outboard motor, but all it did was sputter and die. He tried several more times, with the same result. By now, the wind had picked up considerably, and it began to rain. Waves were breaking over the side of the boat, and we were taking on water.

Sam grabbed the oars and began rowing, while I bailed water as fast as I could. We were making very little headway. We had no life jackets aboard, and neither of us could swim worth a darn. I asked myself how we could have allowed ourselves to get into this mess.

Then, providentially, Sam saw a speedboat heading toward the peer, about 200 yards off our port. We yelled and waved and fortunately caught their attention. Turning their boat, they drew along side. We explained that our motor had died and we were trying to get back to shore. They threw us a rope. Sam secured it to the bow of our small craft, and our good neighbors towed us to safety.

That afternoon Sam got a message from his lawyer that he needed to be back in Chicago the next day for a hearing before the judge. That ended our fishing expedition. Maybe it was just as well.

Another of our roomers was a girl from Japan, whose name I can't remember. Mom abruptly asked her to leave when she found me sharing whiskey highballs with her in the living-room.

There was a salesman fellow, who whistled all the time and who taught me how to play Race Horse Rummy. It's like Gin Rummy but played with seven cards instead of 10.

Then there was Jonatan, a young man from Guatemala and the brother of a lady I'd met through Pompeyo and Esther a year earlier. They got him a job as a dish washer at the El Jarocho Mexican restaurant. He hated it, and after just a few months decided to return to his country.

Jonatan's sister's name was Lidia. She was a nurse at one of the northside hospitals, a petite brunette with dark eyes and a very provocative smile. I never learned how old she was, but she was definitely older and more experienced than I. She knew well how to tease and to flirt. My goal was to make her my conquest. I tried soft music, flattering words and sweet wine but, just when I thought the candle was lit, she'd find a way to extinguish the flame. One New Year's Eve I saved up money and invited her out to a gourmet meal at a fancy restaurant. The evening was going well, and I felt I was making real progress. But the French fried onions I ate began causing me pain and nausea. I hurried home and spent the rest of the night and next morning leaning over or sitting on the toilet. By noon on New Year's Day I was so weak I could hardly crawl out of bed, and that's when Lidia called to invite me to go to the movies. With considerable regret, I had to decline. And that pretty much ended any chance at romance.

A WHITE PHONE AND SHADOW BOXES

For those who don't know, shadow boxes were very popular in homes back in the '50's. They consisted of a series of open irregular wooden shelves used to divide the dining-room area from the living-room. They extended out from the wall perhaps three feet and could go up as high as 6 feet. Ladies loved to place all manner of fragile, porcelain objects on these shelves, and our mom was no exception.

My sleeping area was upstairs in the converted attic, and our only telephone was downstairs in the front hallway, and this presented quite a challenge when I was home alone. I had to race down the attic stairs, dash around our dining-room table past Mom's shadow boxes, through the living-room and into the front hallway to grab the phone before it stopped ringing. Unfortunately, sometimes I swerved a bit off course and there would be a slight crash followed by a tell-tale tin-kling sound. After taking care of the phone call, I'd return on my hands and knees to the scene of the crime to gather up the broken figurines and carry them to the dining-room table where Mom, when she returned, would try and glue them back together one more time, and give me another major scolding.

What could I do to show I really cared about her precious porcelain pieces? And then I had it. A brilliant idea! I would call the phone company and order an extension put upstairs in my bed-room. And, since Mother's Day was just a week away, I would have them replace that ugly black phone in the front hallway with a beautiful new white one. But how much was it going to cost? I had saved up about $15.00. Well, let's call and find out.

Mom in 1955, at age 60, relaxing
following wedding of Eileen Helfenbein,
Dorothy's sister-in-law.

The lady at the phone company was very helpful. She assured me that they could come out the very next day and put in my extension and swap out the old black phone for the new white one. I was thrilled. Mom is going to be so happy. Then I asked her how I would pay for it. "No problem,"

She said, "we'll just add it to your monthly phone bill." Fantastic! I thought. I'll pay Mom back when the bill comes in.

I honestly did have the best of intentions to do so, but somehow my savings got spent on something else. Still, in spite of her grumbling, I think Mom did like the new phone and the fact that I had fewer collisions with her shadow boxes.

WORLD OF WORK

F inding a job when you're a blind teenager or young adult was a major problem back then and still is today. Sighted kids could get jobs as soda jerks, newspaper delivery boys, gas station attendants, dishwashers or busboys in restaurants, stockers, car hops, baby sitters–scores of jobs–and didn't even have to be 16. My brother Jimmy worked at the Rockola girls' softball park when he was 15. Eileen and Dorothy began babysitting when they were just 12 and they were making ice cream sodas and milk shakes at the corner drugstore by age 15. But, because I was blind, those opportunities were not available to me. I did make a few dollars playing my accordion for neighbors, but that felt more like begging for money than earning it.

My first real job was the summer I worked at the Chicago Lighthouse on the assembly line, at 50 cents an hour. We had to be there on time, punch a time clock, take our rest breaks and lunch when the buzzer sounded and keep up our production. It wasn't a job I wanted to do for the rest of my life, but it taught me about work ethic and it put some money in my pocket. One of the items that we made was for the airlines. We made sturdy, plastic lined bags passed out by flight attendants to passengers with queasy stomachs. We playfully referred to them as "whoopy" bags.

I learned how to make hand-made leather belts. I bought the kits from a wholesale store down-town, and I sold them to anyone and everyone I knew. I liked doing that because I was fast, I could set my own hours and I was a pretty good salesman. My profit on each belt was nearly 100%, not a bad return.

The absolute worst job I ever had was as a door-to-door magazine salesman. Paul, Dennis and I were looking for a summer job we could do that would earn us some quick cash. Paul read an ad in the neighborhood newspaper offering "A great chance for bright, intelligent young college students to earn good money".

So, the three of us went to apply. The fast-talking company recruiter told us we could easily make $20.00 to $30.00 a day knocking on doors and giving a foolproof sales pitch to the lady of the house to subscribe to one or more magazines which the company sold. We were skeptical, but it was worth a try, and the company rep didn't seem to care that the three of us were visually impaired.

Along with four other fresh recruits, we were driven to an upscale residential neighborhood on the far north side of Chicago. Getting out of the station wagon, we were rehearsed on what we should say and how to overcome possible objections. We practiced our parts several times until the team leader was satisfied. Then, he gave each of us an order book, a few sample magazines and turned us loose. I found my way to the door of the first house and rang the bell. After a wait, a guy with a gruff voice answered. "Wadaya want?" I started to recite my message. "Not interested!" Slam.

Second house. A sweet old lady told me in broken English she didn't do much reading. At the third house, I was greeted by the barking of a mean-sounding dog. Fourth house, no answer to my incessant ringing. Fifth house, "We already have too many magazines". Sixth house, "I never buy from door-to-door salesmen." Seventh house, "I work nights, and you woke me up." And so it went for the next two hours. Not a single sale.

It was now noon and the temperature was close to 100. Turning the corner, I came across Dennis and Paul. "How you guys doing?" I asked.

"Nothing" they replied. "Not a single sale." Grunts of discouragement and disappointment.

"Hey look," Paul said. "There's a Walgreens drugstore across the street. Wadaya say we go have an iced cold coke?"

"A great idea," Dennis and I agreed.

Once inside the cool, air-conditioned atmosphere of Walgreens, there was little motivation to go back out to face the July heat. "So, any of you guys wanna knock on some more doors?" I asked.

"Not me." Said Paul.

"No thanks," echoed Dennis.

"Then what'll we do with these order books and magazines?" I questioned.

"Let's just give 'em back."

"Who's gonna do it?"

"Since Paul got us into it, I think he should do it." Dennis said. Paul agreed, and that was the end of our short careers as door-to-door salesmen.

I liked telephone sales a whole lot more. First of all, because I did it inside, not exposed to the weather. Secondly, I didn't have to worry about trying to negotiate uneven sidewalks, climbing up porch steps, running into bushes, tripping over flower pots or dealing with barking (maybe biting) dogs. Thirdly, the people I talked to over the phone didn't know I was blind.

My first telephone sales job was with the Chicago Sun Times newspaper. We worked on a commission basis, selling new subscriptions. We were told to say the paper would give a donation to cancer research if the person signed up for a subscription. It sounded almost philanthropic. I don't know how much the Sun Times actually donated, but my conscience was clear. I was helping cancer research and making a few dollars for myself, so I didn't have to keep asking for money from my mom.

Our prospect lists were taken from the City Street Guide. Each night the sales manager would hand me several pages of names with phone numbers. I'd go home and have Mom or one of my sisters tape record the lists which I then brailled to use to make my calls the next night. Instead of my real name, I used my two middle names, Dan Peters, when making my calls, just in case I called someone who might happen to know me. For the most part though, people were pretty nice, and I enjoyed talking with them. Now, however, there are far too many companies using telemarketers, who are calling at all hours, and even I get annoyed and hang up on them.

My second telephone sales job was in Evanston with a heating and air conditioning company that my mom worked for as office manager. I went in the evenings, from 6:00 to 9:00 P.M. Our pitch was to offer the prospect a "free inspection" of their furnace, by our authorized technicians, to ensure the furnace would pass safety standards and not cause problems for the home owner when the fall season began. Of course, once the technicians got a look at the furnace, they usually found some small or large repair or improvement to recommend. They might even make a full system sale. I was paid a commission on the number of appointments I was able to set up, and I did quite well.

NEW HORIZONS

I was 23, graduated from Northwestern and working in radio, which had been my career goal. But, I was not happy. My 30-minute weekly program on WEAW had a loyal but limited audience. The station's signal was not very powerful, and station management did little to promote my show. My earnings were meager, and my future seemed bleak. I felt frustrated, dispirited and full of doubt.

What could I do to change my situation? Should I give up radio and work full-time as a telephone salesperson? Should I go work at the Lighthouse like some of my friends had done? Maybe I ought to become a food stand operator like Bob Turek. None of these ideas appealed to me.

I wanted something more, some sort of new challenge–an opportunity to prove to myself and to my family, especially to my mom , that I was capable of success. Mom never suggested that I give up radio. She knew how much I loved it, and she had faith in me and in my future, more than I did myself. It was for her that I decided I needed to do something to make her proud of me.

Larry at age 25, and Mom, standing
on the front porch on Lawndale. In
background part of a neighbor's house.
View is looking north. October, 1958.

I had made two trips to Mexico as a tourist–the first one when I was 18 and the second three years later. I loved it–the people, the food, the culture. My Spanish was much improved, and I had made some good friends there. Perhaps, I thought, perhaps I could go live in Mexico for a year or two, and if I really learned the language well, I could find a new career as an interpreter or translator or something. Also, I thought, if I were there in Mexico, I wouldn't be under the scrutiny of friends or my family in Chicago. I would be free to be myself, to make mistakes, to learn and, hopefully, to succeed.

A friend told me about a small, American college, located on the outskirts of Mexico City, that offered a graduate program in Latin American Studies. This sounded perfect, a way for me to get out of Chicago, to make a new start. Could I do it? Mom had always said, if you want something bad enough, nothing can stop you.

So, I started the wheels turning. I went back to Mexico in the spring of 1957 and submitted my application to the school. I was accepted and began my exciting new life as an American abroad in September of 1957. That period of my life is described in my earlier book, "Mexico by Touch: True Life Experiences of a Blind American Deejay." My decision to go to Mexico definitely changed my life and introduced me to a whole new world.

Larry Dorothy, Eileen and Jim at Dorothy's home in Parkridge, following death of Mom in 1970.

EPILOGUE

S ince leaving Chicago, more than 50 years ago, I've made many visits back home –to spend Christmas holidays, visit family and friends, celebrate birthdays and attend funerals. Well, of course, it isn't really home anymore, but then again it is. It's the place where I grew up. It's where my roots are. It's full of familiar smells and sounds and tastes that reawaken the memories of my youth–the dreams, the doubts, the desires, the disappointments. But it's also where I will always find a haven of love.

My big sister, Dorothy, and ten families of nieces and nephews shower me with attention and affection on my every visit. It's wonderful to go home, from time to time, and reconnect with people, places and memories.

But much is not the same. The old house on Montrose has had a face lift and is now flanked by two tall apartment buildings. No more open prairie. The candy store is now a real estate office. The grandstands and green expanse of Rock-ola Stadium have been replaced with commercial and residential development. Radio station WEAW has vanished from the airways. Even Wilbur Wright College has been moved and totally transformed from a modest one-building junior college campus on Austin Avenue to a beautiful and modern multi-campus institution at Narragansett and Montrose.

Nor am I the same restless, impatient, naïve young man who left to find his identity and direction in a foreign land so long ago, and that is good. I have so much to be grateful for, not just for where my journey has taken me or for those dreams that have been realized, but even more, for whom I have met along the way. Human relationships provide the most meaningful and lasting imprints on our psyche. We are who we are, due largely to the relationships and human encounters that have been a part of our lives—our family, teachers, friends and strangers.

I am truly fortunate that I had a mother who was endlessly optimistic in the face of adversity, so incredibly intuitive in knowing how to raise a blind child and so single-mindedly dedicated to the happiness and well-being of her family. Her values and her example shaped many of my goals and ideals.

I hope that you have enjoyed this chance to glimpse Inside My World, and to realize that you and I are, in so many ways, alike and yet in others, so very different. It is our uniqueness as individuals that makes our existence so precious. Cherish who you are. Cherish your family. Cherish your friends. Respect and appreciate the abilities and potential of every human being. And, live each day with joy by bringing hope and love and joy to others.

ABOUT THE AUTHOR

L arry P. Johnson is a native of Chicago, graduate of Northwestern University's School of Speech in Evanston, Illinois, with a Master's in Latin American Studies, from La Universidad de las Americas in Mexico City.

His professional background includes:

- 22 years as a radio and television broadcaster in Mexico City, Chicago and San Antonio. He was the first blind newscaster on Mexican television.
- 28 years as a motivational speaker and workshop presenter - having presented for audiences in Mexico, Japan and the United States.
- 21 years as a Human Resources manager with AT&T Communications.

He makes his home now in San Antonio, TX, enjoys tandem bicycling, bowling and reading. He is the father of 6 children and grandfather of 20.

Also author of

- Mexico By Touch: True Life Experiences of a Blind American Deejay, an inspirational account of his adventures and misadventures living and working in Mexico for 17 years and

"You Can If You Think You Can, Rebound From Adversity and Follow Your Dreams", an easy-to-read guide that offers simple strategies to overcome failure, restore self-esteem and achieve success and happiness in your life.